CW00796534

# MARCOS -
# THE STORY OF A GREAT BRITISH SPORTSCAR

## A light-hearted account of an enduring marque and of Jem Marsh, its founder

### The only authorised account of the Marcos story

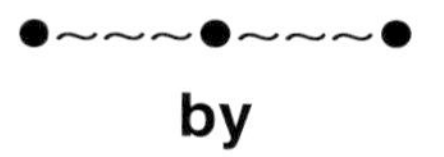

by

David M. Barber

Cedar
Publishing
Limited

Exclusively distributed by Rubicon Studios Limited
24, Bridge Street
Bradford-on-Avon
Wiltshire BA15 1BY
Telephone 01225 868569

The publishers would like to acknowledge the following for the use of their photographs (the source is included with each photograph): *Autosport* (Haymarket Publications) *Bath Chronicle & Herald*, Harold Barker, James Brymer, *Edinburgh Evening News*, John Gaisford, Graham Gauld, Geoffrey Goddard, E. Jelinek, Photo Beroul-Le Mans, Presse Diffusion Lausanne, Fred Scatley, H.P. Seufert, Temple Press Limited, D.I. Tuddenham, *Western Morning News*



ISBN 0 9517002 9 4

Published by Cedar Publishing Limited, Newnham-on-Severn
Gloucestershire

Printed and bound in Great Britain by Butler & Tanner Limited, Frome, Somerset, from recycled Marcos cars

# MARCOS -
# THE STORY OF A GREAT BRITISH SPORTSCAR

## ≈CONTENTS≈


| | | |
|---|---|---|
| | INTRODUCTION | 1 |
| 1 | THE EARLY YEARS | 5 |
| 2 | JEM'S PASSION FOR CAR BUILDING AND MOTOR SPORT IS FIRED | 11 |
| 3 | THE BIRTH OF SPEEDEX | 23 |
| 4 | FRANK COSTIN, DENNIS ADAMS AND THE GULLWING - MARCOS IS BORN | 29 |
| 5 | COMMANDER GREVILLE CAVENDISH, RN (RETIRED) | 50 |
| 6 | THE MARCOS 1800 ARRIVES | 65 |
| 7 | FROM VOLVO TO FORD. THE BRADFORD FLOOD | 84 |
| 8 | THE XP MANTIS AND SPA-FRANCORCHAMPS | 88 |
| 9 | DEBACLE AT LE MANS LEADS TO THE FIRST BIG-ENGINED PRODUCTION MARCOS | 94 |
| 10 | THE MINI MARCOS, LE MANS AND 'FLIRT' | 106 |
| 11 | THE PHOENIX RISES AGAIN: THE '50s DREAM STORMS INTO THE '90s | 120 |
| 12 | JEM MARSH, THE MAN | 139 |
| 13 | THE FUTURE | 146 |
| | APPENDIX - MARCOS ABROAD | 153 |

## Foreword by Jem Marsh

'Many of my friends over the years have suggested that I should write a book about Marcos and I have been approached by several journalists with the same idea. I first started to think seriously about doing this during late '70s and early '80s but not being a 'scholar' I never really knuckled down and put pen to paper. I also was concerned that someone else writing on my behalf would not accurately record what I wanted to say. Although, at one stage, a draft was written, it went no further. Then I met David Barber, a businessman, freelance writer and Marcos owner and the idea of a book finally reached fruition.

'Rightly or wrongly, I made a decision not to include reams of historical facts and figures such as chassis numbers, what engine was fitted when and all the other technical facts which are often found in a book of this type. I wanted a book to be enjoyed by the layperson. If anyone does want more technical information, this is readily available from various other sources already.

'So much has happened over the years with so many good stories that I have been able to include only a small number which I thought would be of interest to readers. David has written the book as if the whole of Marcos revolves around me but there are endless friends, suppliers, competitors, wives and family who have helped me over the years to build up Marcos into an international marque. I apologise to anyone whom I have left out and hopefully another book will follow to bring the stories and the history up to date.

'There are so many people to whom I could dedicate this book, all of whom have helped tremendously. I would first like to dedicate it to the memory of Anton de la Rue, who helped me to build my first car and thus excited my interest. But I don't think that anyone close to the Marcos story would disagree that the three outstanding contributors have been Dennis Adams for his fabulous designs and his continuous support over the years; Greville Cavendish, who supported the company in so many ways during the '60s; and Philip Hulme, who has ensured that the marque will continue well past the year 2000. Last, but not least, my thanks go to my long suffering wife, Lyn, who has been the real driving force behind this book.'

Jem Marsh. Westbury, 1995

# *INTRODUCTION*

When I first approached Jem Marsh to write a book about his creation, the Marcos, it was as the result of the fulfilment of a boyhood dream to own one of these incredibly exciting cars. Little did I know that I was to be privileged to record a much more substantial and intriguing story than the mere history of a marque, for this is an account of a man unique in the British Isles. Jem is still the motivating force behind a British sportscar which is as competitive and alive today as it was when he launched it, 35 years ago.

That is a great record in its own right but what makes it unique is that Marcos Cars Limited is the only car manufacturing company, still at the forefront of motor sport and British sportscar design, which has remained in the same hands all that time: those of Jem Marsh. To put into perspective just how much of a challenge this achievement has been, the advances in motor car performance have been so great since Marcos was launched that many quite modest saloons of today would give a hard time to some of the road going sportscars of 1960.

Leaving aside the question of proprietorship, few road-going sportscars in the world have remained competitive in both road going and racing terms over a 35 year period and this puts the company in the same bracket as Porsche, Ferrari, Lamborghini and Lotus. As has been proven time and time again, this is one car you can realistically use every day for work and at the weekend blow the competition away on the circuits.

Yet how many people know a Marcos and, of those who do, how many know that this great little company is still thriving, now producing cars greater than they have ever been? The fact is that Marcos is the unsung hero of British sportscar manufacture, well able to hold its own against the Italian and German exotics.

●~~~●~~~●

The first recognisably shaped Marcos, the Gullwing, appeared in 1959. These cars were used almost exclusively for competition and very successful they were. First season out, in 1961, with no testing done at all, the first model was driven to 10 wins in 10 races by Bill Moss. Overseas customers, too, have had great success, winning at, among others, the Nürburgring. Marcos also came close to victory in the Japanese Grand Prix (since when the Japanese have been great customers for Marcos). However, the first production model to really catch the public imagination was the famous wooden-chassised 1800, launched in 1964. Powered by a Swedish Volvo engine, it proved highly competitive and won many events.

In 1994, 34 years on from those early racing successes, the company has launched the Marcos LM500. Unbelievably, with only three months of development and with none of the massive resources of the mighty Porsche empire, this unturbocharged car, in the hands of Chris Hodgetts and Jem's son Chris, was already notching up outright wins, beating even the turbocharged Porsches and proving that, after all these years, Jem is still a giant-killer, able to produce cars capable of taking on bigger, far better funded companies - and still win.

Jackie Stewart, one of the greatest racing drivers ever, was among many who started their racing careers in a Marcos. Derek Bell, five times winner of the Le Mans 24 Hours and twice World Sportscar Champion, was another, as was Jonathan Palmer. On current form, there is nothing to suggest that a future 'Jackie Stewart' might not also choose a Marcos in which to start their racing career at the end of this decade - 40 years after Jackie's time. Few would deny that Jem, with his incredible ability to keep bouncing back time after time, has not earned that right more than any other car constructor in the world, never mind Great Britain.

The British were once famous for their indomitable spirit but that, as a national characteristic, is long since gone. Of our once great British motorcyle industry, only Triumph still flies the Union Jack, tenaciously holding on with little help from public or government. The rest gave up almost without a struggle. We once had a great British car industry, too, but it has fared little better. Precious little remains in British hands and the Marcos is one of the few genuinely British cars left of which British people can be truly proud. Indeed, Jem Marsh himself is proud to be British; not only do the works racers display the Union Jack but the company's logo and badge is in red, white and blue colours. But, sadly and typically of British people, we underrate what is truly great about Great Britain and the company undoubtedly does have great market potential. Its bigger-engined cars are already more than a match in terms of appeal, luxury finish and performance for Porsche and Ferrari but, while people with no interest in cars can recognise Ferraris or Porsches, it is only enthusiasts who know about Marcos. The Mini Marcos, too, could sell well. It was the first 'hot hatch' yet still has considerably more personality, individuality and panache than its competitors with the bonus of a far better competition record.

They say that one of the best tests of the quality of a car is its resale price. If that is so, Marcos cars must be near the top of the tree. Even during the recession of the early 1990s, they held consistently high second hand values, often more than they cost the purchaser in the first place. This is not something which can be said of the exotica which come readily to the minds of most people.

What turns a person or an event into a legend is not only that apocryphal stories circulate about them but that no one cares whether they are true or not. As a writer, I often found it difficult to separate fact from fiction where both Jem and the Marcos story are concerned but then does it matter whether a story is objective memory or merely how a person wants to remember something or someone important to them?
One of my problems in writing this book is that there has actually been too much to write about. Jem's life has been packed with so much action, anecdote and humour; the list of Marcos successes is so long (indeed, so numerous are they both in the UK and abroad that many are not even known to the company); and the birth and construction of each model has so much trauma and incident surrounding it, that I have been able to do no more than touch on the whole story.

●~~~●~~~●

The publication of this book marks perhaps the greatest year in both Jem's life and the 35 year history of Marcos to date for four reasons. First, the company has obtained type approval; this does not make the car any better but the public thinks it does and this perception has to be important to the company's future. Second, the launch of the LM500 proves that, after 35 years, the company can still do it. This car could prove to be the greatest Marcos yet on both track and road. Third, 1994 marked a new era in Jem's personal life with his marriage to Lyn, perhaps the one person capable of taming him! Fourth, with the return of his son Chris to the company, the Marsh family is now in its third generation of successful competition drivers, a record rarely equalled in the history of motor sport.

Many people, who know far more than I about Marcos, have played an important part in bringing this book to life. I am very grateful to Lyn who had the very devil of a job in keeping Jem's mind on the project and for coming up with ideas, constant rereading of the drafts and overseeing the publication; to Per Haegermark of Sweden and his Historic Marcos Register for checking the proofs, and to Dennis Adams, the brilliant designer of the Marcos. Per helped in another way, by providing invaluable material, as did Rory McMath and Richard Falconer, the *British* author of the *American* best-selling and definitive book on the Chaparral, and I deeply appreciate the trouble they all went to. I would also like to thank Club Marcos International for some invaluable information and Roger Garland, Secretary of the Mini Marcos Owners' Club, for checking the references and the chapter on the Mini Marcos. Finally, words cannot convey my debt to Marcus Pye, *Autosport* journalist and a very well known figure in motoring circles, for the work he put in on editing this book.

# CHAPTER 1

## THE EARLY YEARS

Jem was born Jeremy George Weston Marsh in Clifton, Bristol, on April 15, 1930. Clifton is one of the nicer parts of Bristol and boasts the largest area of open land within the city boundary. The home of the university; it is now largely populated by the more affluent, interspersed with student accommodation and a wealth of fascinating little shops and restaurants. Built by one of our greatest industrial designers, Isambard Kingdom Brunel, the Clifton suspension bridge dominates the area. One wonders what this great man, so brilliantly unorthodox in his designs and able to make even iron structures look beautiful, would have made of the equally unorthodox but beautiful creations of Marcos. I suspect he would have approved.

Jem's father, Ken, was the third generation of the famous West Country haberdashers who traded under the Marsh name. When Jem chose not to go into the family business, there was no direct line to take over its management and it eventually passed into outside hands.

Ken Marsh was no mean performer in motor sport, mainly in car trials. In those days, these were a mixture of timed sections and modern car trials and consisted of trying to get as far up a steep hill as possible. He won many trophies, mostly in his own Triumph Dolomites although he occasionally drove one of Donald Healey's. His speciality was Beggar's Roost Hill in Somerset and he holds the distinction of being the only driver to have climbed it over 100 times under RAC supervision. The car he used for this, an MG M Type, is now in the MG museum in Abingdon. Beggars Roost was also included in the RAC Rally in 1956, in which Ken competed in a works Jowett Javelin. Even then, not all the cars were able to scale the hill.

***Ken and Marjorie Marsh, Jem's parents, in their Chain-gang Frazer-Nash***

Jem's parents were divorced in 1940. His mother was married again in 1946 to Anton de la Rue, the last male heir of that famous business dynasty.

•~~~•~~~•

On the day war was declared, September 3, 1939, Jem had his tonsils out. When he got home, an infection persisted and he was diagnosed as having tuberculosis. In those days, continuous fresh air was the recognised treatment and so, during a bitterly cold spell, he lived day and night in a tent in the garden. Another part of the treatment was two pints of boiled milk a day, something which his mother found great difficulty in administering. Anyway, after two months of camping out, his grandfather, E.G. Marsh, took pity on him and replaced the tent with a revolving summer house, in which Jem stayed for the next 10 months. It was then discovered that what had been identified as tuberculosis was not that at all, but a shadow on one lung which eventually disappeared of its own accord.

Jem went to Wycliffe College, a well known public school based at Stonehouse in Gloucestershire. He had already lost a year of schooling due to the misdiagnosed illness and this, aggravated by being taught by conscientious objectors who made little attempt to make him work, meant that he was never able to catch up. The result was that he spent more time enjoying himself than studying. It was war time and the college had moved to Lampeter in mid Wales. Fishing there was good, gamekeepers were scarce due to the war, and there was a ready market for salmon in the surrounding area........
After the war, the college moved back to its home in Gloucestershire. There, in an old boathouse by a weed-choked canal, Jem and his friends found some canoes which had been locked away during the hostilities. For Jem, this sparked off an interest in boats and their construction.
Against all school rules, one of his friends had a 600cc flat-twin Douglas motorcycle. The temptation for Jem was too great. Here was the perfect expression of his need for freedom as he hurtled around Gloucestershire untaxed and uninsured. It was only a question of time before he was caught. Although he was only 16½, his parents (or perhaps it was the headmaster?) realised the futility of him staying at school any longer.

***Boy-Seaman Jem Marsh, known as Lofty. HMS St. Vincent, 1946***

To Jem, it seemed logical to progress from canoes on a canal to ships at sea, so he spent the next nine and a half years in the Royal Navy, starting with a year's boy seaman training on HMS St. Vincent in Gosport and ending with a spell in Plymouth. Between these times, he served with the Mediterranean Fleet commanded by Lord Louis Mountbatten. HRH Prince Philip was for a time in the same flotilla, as captain of HMS Magpie. The natural step for an ex-public schoolboy would have been officer training but Jem turned down the opportunity because this would have meant signing up for a longer period, and he was not convinced that he wanted a career in the Navy. Even so, quality will out; without any apparent effort, and despite the extra-curricular activities which we will cover later, Jem became the youngest Petty Officer in the Mediterranean Fleet at that time. However, his decision not to go for a commission also meant forgoing officer's pay, something he needed to finance a lifestyle which was not possible on a rating's income. Among other activities which shall remain untold - but which can, with Jem's obvious zest for living, be guessed at - he missed the excitement of his school friend's Douglas and wanted a motorcycle.

The opportunity to make the extra money he sought came when he was made official Ship's Photographer. It did not take him long to develop this into a lucrative side-line.

***Jem on a friend's 1000cc HRD Vincent Rapide in Malta***

Using Naval resources of course, he soon realised the potential in taking photographs of the Mediterranean and selling them to his ship mates to send home to their loved ones. As soon as he could, he bought a motorcycle - a Triumph Speed Twin with a sprung hub, which was a devil to ride. This nearly proved the death of him. As Jem recalls: 'I had an accident by skidding on some gravel. I shot over the handlebars and landed on my head. Everyone thought I was dead and it was only when they got me to the local hospital - a Maltese one - that they realised there was still some life in me. The last thing the Maltese authorities wanted was all the bureaucracy of a dead non-civilian on their hands so, despite my critical condition, they threw me out as quickly as they could, into a Naval hospital.

'I was lucky. The only real damage was a broken shoulder blade. I quickly got very bored in hospital so I arranged for my motorcycle to be repaired - all it suffered was bent front forks - and I went absent without leave from the ward for a ride. Unfortunately, the ward sister saw me riding one-handed round Malta, with my arm in a sling. So, when I tried to sneak back into my bed, I was confronted by a vengeful harridan waiting for me. She was so angry, she sent me straight back to my ship.'

It may well have been Jem who introduced crash helmets to Malta. Up to then, no one there had bothered with head protection (few people in the UK did, either). But his accident made him think again and he got his mother to send out a Corker helmet. His lead was soon copied by other people on the island and one of the first things Jem did when he started going out with Barbara Chinn, then a Wren and later to become his first wife, was to get a helmet sent over for her. It is little known among members of the public and even, unfortunately, among followers of motor sport, that one of the things which sets the genuine competition driver apart from the pseudo-racer on a public road is a commitment to safety. Later, Marcos was the second car company to be certified as conforming to the Society of Motor Manufacturers and Traders' (SMMT) Code of Practice for component cars. This required rigorous standards of engineering testing including safety belts and their mountings.

***Jem uses the only mode of transport to visit the lost city of Petra, 1952***

# CHAPTER 2

## *JEM'S PASSION FOR CAR BUILDING AND MOTOR SPORT IS FIRED UP*

There was not much sign of the direction Jem's future life was to take in those early years. Bearing in mind that we are talking of a time when most schoolboys knew - even if they did not like - what their future held for them, there seemed to be an aimlessness about him, a restlessness with no object. Although the Royal Navy had been his choice, he did not convince even himself that it was the right one. He did have an apparent interest in motorcycles, but it was the outlet for a restless and zestful spirit which motorcycles gave him, not motorcycles in themselves, which attracted him. In fact, before he left Malta, he ordered a motorcycle to await his return to England. But he changed his mind as soon as he got back here.

You would think that he inherited his interest in cars and his passion for motor sport from his father, but Jem insists not. His active interest did not start until after he was posted back to the UK and Jem says that the person who really influenced him was his stepfather, Anton de la Rue. Although he did not take part in competition himself, Anton loved cars. He had taken the unusual step, for someone from his wealthy background, of going through a Rolls Royce apprenticeship. During the war, he was a hydraulics engineer and had designed the hood for the Austin A90. His own cars were Bugattis and Lancia pillarless saloons - the Lancia at that time was seen as a thoroughbred motor car, a reputation which it has lost since although the new models look set to re-establish its standing.
It was Anton who taught Jem to drive, using one of his own Austin Sevens. It was also with Anton that Jem went to buy his first car, a partly-built Austin 750 special bought with money saved from his ship's photographer's business.

***Jem's first car, built during his Naval service in 1953. Before..............***

***..............and after!***

The car was near Brooklands and it was just a chassis with the suspension in bits. Only the Austin side rails were in place and the suspension medium was heavy, bungee-like elastic, similar in design to the earlier Kieft 500cc rear engined racing car. 'The trouble with this suspension', says Jem, 'was that it was attached with jubilee clips. The elastic had a habit of pulling out periodically, which meant roadside repairs involving looping the elastic between double wishbones and round aluminium pulleys.'

With Anton's help, Jem built the car at Anton's home in Inkpen, near Newbury. At this time, he was still in the Navy, stationed at Plymouth. After the car was completed, he took it down to his ship and used it there for daily transport. Shortly afterwards, he married Barbara and this was their honeymoon car. Jem also used it for weekend trips to Bath. It was on one of these trips, to a friend's wedding at Bath Abbey, that Jem had his second road accident. 'I hit a lorry head-on in Radstock,' he explains. 'So I ended up in hospital again, this time with internal haemorrhages

and a broken leg. But the pain in my left foot and ankle was so bad that eventually they had to take the plaster off, only to find that the doctor had failed to notice that my foot had been badly scalded. It had gone through the bulkhead of the car and water from the block had burned it so severely that I needed three skin grafts.
'While I was in hospital, the Navy lost me in their records - I didn't hear from them once! By this time, my father had left the family business and had taken the Red Lion pub at Woolverton, near Bath. So, when the hospital discharged me, and as the Navy had clearly forgotten about me, I decided to stay with him and rebuild my 750 special. I found an agricultural engineer to help me. As the front end was damaged, I took the opportunity to convert the front suspension from those damned elastics to a transverse leaf spring. But I still retained the elastic at the rear because that did not give much trouble.'

●~~~●~~~●

It was now 1954 and the president of the Bristol Motor Club found himself short of a car for the 750 team which he had entered for the three-hour relay race at Silverstone. He made enquiries of the 750 Motor Club and it was through it that he made contact with Jem.
Jem remembers that fateful meeting very well because it fired the passion for motor racing which has stayed with him to the present day. 'The president of the club came out to see me at my father's pub, accompanied by a whole flock of Austin Sevens taking the opportunity for a day out. Father was very proud of his immaculate courtyard and he was not best pleased to see these Austin Sevens dripping oil all over it. He was even less pleased when all their owners drank was half pints of bitter instead of the gin and tonics which were then the fashion!'
Despite his father's interest in motor sport, Jem at this stage knew nothing at all about it. He had watched only one meeting, at Castle Combe, and, although he still remembers Ken Wharton in a BRM V16 roaring round that circuit (and who could forget the wail of that car in full flight?), he had not yet followed it up. The president of the Bristol Motor Club explained to Jem that, before he went any further, he must pass a medical. The fact that Jem was still on crutches from his accident did not concern the president at all.

All Jem needed to do, he said, was to find a doctor who did not know him and bluff his way through.
'I took my crutches to the doctors and left them in the car,' remembers Jem, 'and went in trying very hard not to limp. All went well for a while, as he tested my pulse and all that nonsense. But then he asked me to stand on tiptoe and jump from one foot to the other. I did it - I am not sure how - but all he could say was, "Do you know, *I* can't do that. I've got a gammy right foot, you know!"'
As was habitual in those days, Jem had to drive the long distance to Silverstone for the event. He almost did not make it. The Austin Seven magneto had failed earlier and Jem, together with his agricultural engineer friend, had bolted on a great, bulky tractor one in its place.

***Jem in his first car in his very first race, the Silverstone Three Hour Relay Race, 1954. He broke the endurance record in this race, a record he holds to this day***
(Courtesy Harold Barker)

What they failed to realise was that it was not designed to take the much higher revs of the Austin engine. The resultant heat build-up had caused the shellac in the armature to melt, inevitably resulting in a dead engine. Although it seemed quite pointless, he went ahead with a roadside repair and scraped all the melted gunge out. To his amazement, it worked and the car got him to Silverstone on time.
Jem was so green that he knew nothing about scrutineering, the need for race numbers and so on. In those days, there were no such thing as sticky numbers: they were actually painted onto the cars for the drivers.
Jem's reputation for building fast, reliable cars started at that race meeting. Although it was a four car team for a three hour race, the other three cars all blew up, leaving Jem to drive for two and a half hours on his own. This did not bother him one bit because he revelled in every second of it. His enduring memory of that day, apart from his own excitement, was of Denis Jenkinson driving a Porsche 356. 'Jenks' was well known as Stirling Moss's co-driver for Mercedes-Benz in the 1955 Mille Miglia, that famous road race down the length of Italy. However, Jem set a record, in this, his first race, which stands to this day: the greatest number of laps by a single 750 car in the Silverstone Three Hour Relay Race. (He was later to break the record for the greatest number of laps driven by one driver in the Silverstone Six Hour Relay Race)

By now, Jem felt that the Navy had lost him for long enough and that he had better reintroduce himself before someone discovered him missing in their records - not that, in the event, it made much difference to his life. He and Barbara were living in a caravan just outside Plymouth. Next to the caravan was a barn in which Jem continued to indulge his new-found passion for building Austin Seven specials, apparently virtually unhindered by naval duties.
'I had a crowd of young chaps down there,' he remembers, 'who used my barn to build their own cars. We could pick up Austin Sevens for £5. I suppose, today, similar cars would set you back at least £4,000! The Navy taught me how to weld and how to work aluminium, so we used those skills to build our own bodies out of aluminium and tubing.'

●~~~●~~~●

In 1955, aged 25, Jem decided to call it a day in the Navy. Although it clearly made little demand on his time, he now wanted to spend all his time with cars and the obvious future seemed to be in car sales. It is an interesting window on attitudes at the time that, although Jem was ex-public school and obviously from the same background as the officers, the fact that he was not an officer meant that the careers adviser had him down for a future as a welder.

'Good heavens!' Jem said. 'I only learnt that so that I could build Austin Seven specials!'

'What are your plans, then?' asked the careers guidance officer. Jem explained that he already had a job offer from W. Mumford to sell cars.

'Are you really capable of that?' queried the officer. As Jem puts it, 'Officers thought everyone not at their level was thick!'

In the event, that officer was closer to the truth than he realised, although not for the right reasons.

***Tren Wainton Hill Climb, 1954. Jem with his 750 Special breaks the record and wins his class*** (Courtesy James Brymer)

Jem had expected that the job would give him all the time he wanted to devote to his twin passions of car building and competition but he found he had nowhere near the freedom which the Navy had allowed him and in fact was rarely able to find time to do more than a few hill climbs. However, his reputation for uninhibited driving was still gaining momentum. Less than a year later, he was approached by Gerry Scali, the proprietor of a travelling car stunt team called the Hollywood Motor Maniacs and European Motor Rodeo. The name must have been chosen because no one came from America and they did not get to Europe.

GERRY SCALI

PRESENTS

EUROPEAN MOTOR RODEO

Directed by GEORGE COAKER

*(Management reserves the right to omit, alter sequence of events or substitute any number at its own discretion)*

**PART 1**

1. GRAND PARADE ... *Jock Maxwell, Paddy Power, Carl Kentner, Dave Watts, Rod Marsh, Colin Moore*
2. PRECISION DRIVING
3. FLAME SLIDE ... ... ... ... *Fred Easton*
4. OVERTAKING THE HARD WAY *Rod Marsh and Carl Kentner and Pat Ryder on the Trapeze*
5. COPS AND ROBBERS ... ... ... *Wait and See*
6. PIT STOP ... ... *Dave Watts in Car, Rod Marsh and Paddy in the Pits*
7. SUICIDE RIDE ... ... *Paddy Power and Fred Easton*
8. THE CRASH ROLL ... ... ... ... *Dave Watts*
9. LOOP THE LOOP ... ... ... *Jock Maxwell*

INTERVAL

**PART 2**

10. CRAZY CAR, CRAZY MAN ... ... ... *Tich*
11. FLAMING BARRIER ... ... ... ... *Pat Ryder*
12. TWO WHEEL BALANCE ... ... ... *Dave Watts*
13. DIVE BOMBER SMASH ... ... *'Lucky' Fred Easton*
14. PRECISION DRIVING
15. Tich Again
16. THE HIGH LEAP ... ... *Dave Watts and Jock Maxwell*
17. **FINALE**

*London Press and Public Relations Office* : GREENWOOD, RITCHIE & MORRIS .. MUSEUM 2580

*Agents* .. WALLABY INTERNATIONAL VARIETY & CIRCUS AGENCY .. PLYMOUTH 60426

***The European Motor Rodeo's crazy programme of events, 1955.......***

He could not resist the challenge. There were six drivers in the team, all driving Mark I Ford Zodiacs. For the purposes of authenticity, they were given American names although Jem's did lack flair: Jem Marsh simply became Rod Marsh.

'Apart from the other stunts,' he says, 'we devised my own act incorporating my Austin Seven special and this was called "Overtaking the Hard Way by

Rod Marsh". We bought a Ford V8 Pilot soft top and welded twin ramps onto it. These trailed down behind and the idea was that, instead of overtaking the Ford in the normal fashion, I would drive up and over it. To make it more exciting, a trapeze was welded to the top of the Ford and, as I went through, the boss's girlfriend would drop from it onto the passenger seat of the special.

'The ramps used to flap along the ground which was a bit worrying but, as long as the guy in the Ford didn't go too fast and the twin carburettors of the special were on song, getting up the ramp was not too bad. The problem came at the top because I actually had to stop the special on the moving Ford to let the trapeze artiste drop into my car. The trouble was that Austin Sevens, even those modified for racing, had completely unreliable cable brakes. It was almost impossible to get the car to pull up under hard braking in a straight line - you never knew which way they would pull. That was not such a problem for me on the ramps; the far worse one was that cable brakes were not very good at stopping cars anyway. The only way I could stop that special on top of the Ford was to, literally, stand up on the brake pedal and at the same time grab the upright supports of the trapeze as they went by! There were, of course, times when I missed. The car would go crashing on and I would have to come round for another go. The crowd used to love that!

'The next problem was that the trapeze artiste had to aim pretty accurately. Not only were those Austins tiny by today's standards but everything was hard-edged steel or aluminium and, to cap it all, there was no proper seat to land in!

'As if that wasn't enough, her extra weight was enough to bend the front axle beam on landing so, after each show, I had to get the welding torch out to straighten it. Fortunately, the petrol tank was nowhere near.......

'My wife Barbara was also in the show. Her job was to stand on the bonnet of one of the Mark I Zodiacs, specially equipped with a rail, and, dressed in a cowgirl outfit, parade round the town to publicise the evening's entertainment. But we had to call a halt to this when she became pregnant with our first child.'

***'Overtaking the hard way'. Note Jem's pseudonym - 'Rodeo Rod'! Jem's car, suitably modified, is the first 750 Special he built and is the same as that raced at Silverstone*** (Courtesy *Western Morning News*)

***Jem, alias 'Rodeo Rod', completes his overtaking manoeuvre. Pat Ryder is on the trapeze and the barely recognisable Ford V8 Pilot soft top is driven by Carl Kentner***
(Courtesy *Edinburgh Evening News*)

David Watts was one of those Zodiac drivers. He has remained friends with Jem ever since and was kind enough to tell me a wealth of stories of that time. Clearly, it was a great time and I wish I had room to tell more than this one: 'One of my acts was to drive the car through a burning hoop of straw with a colleague, Carl Kentner, strapped to the front. Normally we soaked the straw in petrol but, on this occasion we were short of money so we decided on paraffin, which was much cheaper. Now, paraffin does not burn with the reasonably clear flame of petrol; instead, our burning hoop gave off vast columns of black smoke which covered the whole stadium. I couldn't even see the burning hoop properly so, when we went through, I was slightly off line and hit it. When we emerged into the daylight, there was poor old Carl on the bonnet being grilled in burning straw. Luckily, no damage was done but Carl's terror was all wasted because the crowd were blinded by black smoke and saw nothing.'

(Courtesy *Western Morning News*)

Ellis Dawe, another of the drivers, is now the proprietor of the Dartmoor Wildlife Park. It sounds as if that is where the whole Rodeo should have been.
This was a tremendously enjoyable time in Jem's life but it came to an abrupt end when the Hollywood Motor Maniacs and European Motor Rodeo ran out of money in Yorkshire, and they were all left to find their own ways home. Jem had no idea where to go, so he decided by the simple expedient of sticking a pin in a map. It chose Reading. Actually, this was not such a bad choice because his step father, Anton, had built a modern pig farm nearby, at Inkpen (where Jem had built his first special).
Life at this time was all in caravans. He and Barbara had moved into one as their first marital home. The time he was with the rodeo was naturally all spent in a caravan and now this, parked in a Reading layby, became home for the next few months.
Perhaps the only thing wrong with the rodeo was that it clashed with Jem's enjoyment of racing. With its demise, he was once again able to indulge in that passion. His 750 special was by now no longer competitive and he did not have the funds to make it so; he did not even have enough money to repaint it, so it must have been a splendid sight as it raced the circuits in the rodeo colours of red, white and blue stripes.

His first job after the rodeo was a purely stop-gap, one selling combine harvesters, but this soon gave way to something closer to his heart when he became a technical representative for the Firestone Tyre and Rubber Company. This was invaluable not only because he got a company car but because he was able to add greatly to his knowledge of suspension systems.
An offer then came to join Dante The Sporting Motorist Agency as their general manager. This company specialised in making and selling conversions and parts for Austin Seven specials and was obviously ideally suited to Jem's experience - as well as, of course, allowing him to learn even more about his passion for converting cars. Unfortunately, the company was badly under-funded and it collapsed. The time had now come for Jem to run his own show.

# CHAPTER 3

# THE BIRTH OF SPEEDEX

Thus, in 1957, Jem's first company was born, Speedex Castings and Accessories Limited, based in Luton, in a converted hat factory. Jem had just £44 capital and he blew the lot on an advertisement. Fortunately for him, enough sales were generated from it to get the business going. From the start, this company, combining as it did all his enthusiasm for, and experience of, 750 specials, was a success. While the Hollywood Motor Maniacs had been an enjoyable interlude it was never more than a paid holiday. Now, for the first time, Jem was truly at home doing something he really wanted to do. And it showed.

He launched the company with his own design of wishbone suspension and this was quickly followed by a whole host of parts and modifications, all designed to offer a complete service to the 750 and Ford 10 enthusiast. Although the company's initial advertising was geared to attract calling customers, a national mail order business slowly built up.

This was also the year in which the Americans introduced go-karting to Great Britain. Although many purist competition drivers looked down on karts, the more serious specialist car manufacturers saw the opportunity in them. Progress Chassis, which at that time made the chassis for Lotus, had a go-kart ready for one of the first races, held at Mildenhall in Suffolk. Jem came into the market with two models. The bigger one, the Speedex Spree-Kart, was powered by a Villiers engine while the smaller one used the American Clinton motor, a unit designed for chainsaws. Over 60 Speedex go-karts were sold, including 20 to the NAAFI in Cyprus.

***The Speedex Spree-Kart, one of the first Karts to be built in the UK***
(Courtesy Temple Press Ltd)

Speedex also cast and sold hundreds of its own design of wheel, which had to take the only tyre then available to go-karts. Made by Firestone, it was actually intended for wheelbarrows! Jem's one and only race, which included the future Formula 1 double World Champion Graham Hill driving a Progress, was not a happy experience: he turned over and, although heavily bruised, was much more annoyed at ruining a smart, brand new sweater.

The company's success inevitably led to the launch of its own aluminium 'Speedex' open two-seater body for the Austin Seven - inevitable because there had already been considerable demand from enthusiasts for replicas of the body Jem had designed for his own car. To get the body of the first one built out of the factory, they had to remove a window.

***Jem on board the first 750 Speedex body designed for sale, launched in 1958. Photo taken outside the Luton 'hat' factory***

Jem followed this by developing his own 750 Formula racing car, sticking to the aluminium body for the simple reason that, although fibreglass was cheaper, he had not yet learned how to mix it.

Racing success with this new car would put Speedex on the map, so it suddenly became important to get good results on the track. Jem decided that he should try to find expert tuition. As luck would have it, the Cooper Car Company advertised in *Autosport* magazine for aspiring racing drivers to go on its course. The cost was five guineas, and successful applicants would get a works drive in a single-seater Cooper. This sounded just what he needed so he sent off his money. Back came his membership, various rules and instructions and a date on which to attend the course at Brands Hatch. Then a thought occurred to him: would his 6'4" frame actually fit into a Cooper single-seater racing car? After all, five guineas was considerably less than the average weekly income in those days, so it was a lot to lose. He decided to pose that question to John Cooper on the basis that there was not much point in turning up if he could not even get into the car. The honest John Cooper clearly agreed because back came Jem's five guineas.

***Jem winning the 1959 750 Championship in his own car (with, inset, the donor car)***

***...............and collects his winner's spoils from the famous actress, Billie Whitelaw!***

Not started until late 1957, the new Speedex car was nevertheless ready for the 1958 season and it was an immediate success. Continuing the promise he had shown as part of the Bristol Motor Club relay team in 1953, Jem carved straight through the opposition and ended the season as the winner of the Goodacre Trophy for the 750 Formula Championship - a remarkable performance.

It was during this championship that Jem met the current chairman of the 750 Motor Club, Mike Featherstonhaugh. Mike was to win the trophy the following year by designing a bodyshell in fibreglass which allowed for a more aerodynamic shape. A deal was struck for Speedex to market the front and rear body moulds to special builders.

***The 'Silverstone' body shell designed by Mike Featherstonhaugh, which he used to win the 1960 750 Formula Championship***

In 1958, Speedex also made its first move away from the 750s which had, until then, been its stock in trade. Peter Hammond, a local enthusiast, came up with a design for a closed fibreglass coupé based on Ford 100E parts and Speedex collaborated with him on its production. After initial enthusiasm, Jem did not put his customary motivation behind what was named the Speedex Sirocco GT; the result was that only 10 were built. He does however regret not registering that Sirocco name because, under the alternative spelling of Scirocco, the licence for its use could have been sold twice later: to BRM and Volkswagen.

The 750 car market, as with the many home-build conversions which were available at the time, was the result of a swingeing rate of purchase tax imposed on new cars which made it impossible for manufacturers to supply low priced sportscars. As this tax was not levied on home-built cars, it pushed the market into doing what it could with refurbished second hand cars and parts.
In 1959, the government slashed this tax in one move. The Austin-Healey Sprite was the first low-priced sportscar to appear and the resulting sudden freeing of the market flooded it with cheap second-hand cars which cost less than conversions.
Jem had always realised that the Austin Seven conversion market was never going to do other than get by financially but that is not something about which he felt concern; he has always been more interested in doing something fulfilling than in earning money. Had it not been for this change in the tax laws, perhaps he would have been content to stay where he was for ever - and perhaps Marcos would never have been born.

As it was, Speedex was not going to survive and he had to look for something else. As so often happens, just when one does not know what to do next, fate took a hand and Frank Costin appeared on the scene.

# *CHAPTER 4*

## *FRANK COSTIN, DENNIS ADAMS AND THE GULLWING - MARCOS IS BORN*

Frank Costin was a distinguished designer who had done his training with the De Havilland Aircraft Company, where he specialised in aerodynamics and worked extensively on wooden-framed aircraft.
He left to set up his own design consultancy business. Lotus and Vanwall cars, among others, owed much to his design input. His most recent assignment had been to design the spaceframe chassis and body for the Lister Jaguar sports racer. Unfortunately, he devoted too much time to this at the expense of his other business so when, in 1959, his contract with Lister Engineering finished, Frank found he had very little other work left.

Jem was at that time chairman of a branch of the 750 Motor Club, and Frank appeared at a meeting he was holding in a local pub. Although they had not met before, Frank's work with Lotus, Vanwall and Lister had made him legendary in motor racing circles but, in addition, Jem knew of him as the man who had used a wooden chassis in the construction of an Austin Seven based special. The reason this interested Jem particularly was because, since his schooldays, he had worked with wood - a medium he felt much more at home with than steel.

The timing for both men was right and they hit it off at that first meeting. When Jem told Frank that he had a pile of parts in his garage ready to build a Ford-engined car to contest the 1172 Formula racing championship, it seemed a good idea to both men, by now well mellowed in the pub, to go and have a look at them. When they reached Jem's bungalow, he realised that he had not a drink in the place 'except,' he says, 'for a bottle of egg flip, that bloody awful stuff which tastes like custard powder with brandy, eggs

and avocado pear! But Frank was too far gone to care and he polished the lot off while I rummaged around in the garage and eventually came up with a Triumph Herald front suspension, which I brought into the living room.
'Colin Chapman's Lotus Six and Eric Broadley's Lola were at that time the cars to beat but they had severe limitations as road cars. I wanted a top for mine to make it more usable on the road; there were no problems with the racing regulations for this as the 1172 Formula allowed for open or closed bodywork. But the problem would be that, to compete, it would have to be lighter than the Lotus Seven. Frank did not leave until four in the morning, by which time it was decided that the only way to build a road car capable of competing on the track would be to make a wooden monocoque body and chassis unit to accept the mechanical parts I already had in stock.'

Thus was born the Marcos, the name being made up of the first letters of Marsh and Costin. But the company Jem formed to construct it was called the Monocoque Body Chassis Company Limited (MBC) which, almost predictably, became known as the All-to-cock Shoddy and Bashy Company in later years.

Plywood, the medium to be used, has the advantages of being about 50 percent lighter than a conventional steel chassis, with cheapness, cleanliness and exceptional lasting qualities. It is also a very safe material, the wood and fibreglass combination absorbing the shocks of an accident. As Jem explains in bizarre fashion: 'Take two equal sized boxes, one of steel and the other of wood. Now put a mouse in each and hit the boxes with a hammer. The steel box will flatten and squash the mouse; the wooden one will splinter and the mouse usually gets away.' '*Usually?*' The way he explains it, it sounds as if he has tried it more than once!
Accident damage to a wooden chassis is also localised, whereas a shunt with a steel one can distort the entire structure. This means that repairs can be very much less expensive because they are usually confined to replacing the wood and fibreglass in the immediate locality of the collision area. But, of course, it does need a very different set of skills and Frank, after his experience with wooden aircraft, had the experience to apply this element to cars. In use, the structure was to give an endearing 'clunk' as

the suspension came under load and this became a familiar feature to the owners of wooden chassised Marcos.

By the time Jem and Frank reached agreement about the building of the 1172 special, Frank and his wife had moved to Dolgellau in North Wales where his parents-in-law lived. Their agreement was that, while Speedex should finance the project, Frank should build it in North Wales.

One of the engineers with whom Frank had worked at Lister was Dennis Adams. Dennis was to play an integral part in the Marcos story for it was he who, in collaboration with his brother Peter, was to design every model after the first, somewhat unfortunate looking, Frank Costin car. He was the one who brought grace and beauty to the style, and conceived what many people feel is the most beautiful car in the world. It is difficult to understand now, when so many cars are a watered-down version of that shape, the impact of what Dennis did when he produced those first aerodynamically styled bodies.
Dennis is larger than life in both build and character: 14½ stones in weight, with a voice, a personality and a humour to match. He seems able to work only under the motivation of enthusiasm and in two gears: top or neutral. If a project excites him, he will drive himself almost to extinction but, without that motivation, he seems content to do nothing for long periods. He may have come into the company at the behest of, and as second string to, Frank Costin but, while Frank's (albeit integral) contribution was to stop with the wooden chassis and the first all-conquering competition car, it was Dennis who made the continuing contribution to the company's ability, not just to keep up but to lead the field in style and concept. In 1993, McLaren launched, with great publicity, its new concept of a three-seater mid-engined coupé, with a central driver's position. In 1962, Dennis had already designed a similar concept which actually had stylistic and design features McLaren could not match 31 years later! Except for circumstances, that car, the XP, would have gone into production.
Dennis was an ex-RAF man who, as so often happens, took time to find the right occupation after he left the service. For a while, he took a job as a works manager in a factory manufacturing aircraft landing systems. But his main interest was in building specials or, rather, in attempting to build them

because, to him, shape was all-important - so much so that he was constantly dissatisfied with his efforts and therefore, part way through every project, he would scrap it to make way for the next one.
He eventually realised that, until he got the training to match his vision, he was never going to design a car which satisfied him. Close to where he lived, in Cambridge, was Brian Lister's engineering company and he could not have hoped to find a more convenient place to learn. It was here he met and became very friendly with Frank Costin. Dennis's early interest in abstract wood carving and sculpture had given him a fine eye for line but it was only though his association with Frank that he realised how this could be translated into car design. This explained why his own early efforts at building specials had never produced the results he wanted.
After leaving Lister Engineering, Frank promised Dennis that, should any interesting opportunities come his way, he would let him know. When, in late 1959, the 1172 project got off the ground, Frank remembered his promise to Dennis and so it was that Dennis joined the team as works foreman, at the princely salary of £35 per month.
By now Christmas was approaching and, if there was any chance of having the car ready for the new season, it was essential that the new team should forgo the festivities and work right through the holiday.
The intention was that Frank's father-in-law should build a workshop for them in his back garden but, in the meantime, the team had to have premises in which to work. Unsuitable premises were to become one of the hallmarks of Marcos but, even by those standards, the workshop Frank found was basic in the extreme. Behind the Golden Lion Hotel in Dolgellau, it was built as an old coach house and had barely been upgraded since. Even the old block-cobbled flooring sloping down to a central drain was still there and the cold was intense, despite Frank's efforts to lower the ceiling with polythene sheeting.
While Jem was fully committed back at Speedex in Luton, Frank and Dennis started work on the wooden shell of the car. Three weeks later Peter Adams, Dennis's brother, arrived. Peter is a highly skilled and qualified carpenter and it was quickly agreed that he should take on the job of bringing to life Frank's design ideas. The team wanted to design a car which could be both raced competitively and sold for road use.

Some weeks later, the shell was ready to receive its mechanical parts and Jem made the long trip to Dolgellau, the Speedex VW van loaded with parts, to see the car for the first time. Jem describes his first impression: 'It was hideous! Fortunately, I had not expected it to look dreamy. The car was designed for racing and, by that stage, you have lost interest in what it will look like anyway. Your main concern is: will it eat up the opposition? But the way it sat hunched on its trestles peering lop-sidedly at me makes me look back and realise that it was one of the ugliest creatures ever to grace a road!'
Given Frank's commitment to beauty in his other design work, the car seemed to have been a radical departure for him. This car, the Gullwing and the first to bear the Marcos name, actually looked more as if it was designed as it went along and perhaps it was. It had a long, tapering snout, a four piece windscreen and, with its abnormally low bonnet which looked far too shallow to take an engine contrasted with a high cabin to accommodate the 6'4" Jem, resembled a boot. The front wings were cycle-type mudguards and the rear lights stuck out like a frog's eyes. The glue used for all the wooden joints was a product called Aerolite which had been developed during World War II for the Mosquito fighter-bomber. It certainly worked because Jem is still racing one of those early cars today.

Curiously, none of the windows were designed to be opened. As Jem explains: 'Frank did not want them to be opened because they spoilt the aerodynamic flow; he did not really care whether the driver could breathe or not. In early photographs, you can just see a louvre on top which was supposed to duct air down onto the driver. But what he forgot was that, when it rained, the driver would sit in a permanent shower!'

•~~~•~~~•

The team, now up to four people, was really under pressure. The new season was not far away and problems at Speedex meant that Jem could not hang around for long. The car simply had to be completed as quickly as possible so that Jem and Frank could take it back to Luton for completion. They gave themselves 10 days to complete the build and, by working 18 hours a day and more, with breaks only to sleep and eat, they did it. At 3.30 one morning, the little car was run out of its workshop and much to the consternation of the residents of Dolgellau, fired up and given a test run round the town.

***The prototype Marcos 'Ugly Ducking', 1959. Note the missing nose-cone, which was the cure for over-heating. Also the air intake over the windscreen, the only means of getting air to the driver, but which resulted in him getting soaked when it rained!***

After only a few hours' sleep, Frank and Jem rose to start the long trip back to Luton, followed by one of the Speedex mechanics in the van and leaving the rest of the team to a well-earned rest. They had not travelled far before the engine boiled over. Frank had designed the cooling system for the race track and it depended for its efficiency on a high speed being maintained - an impossibility on the twisting Welsh mountain roads. Fortunately, the solution was simple: the nose cone was transferred from the Marcos to the back of the van.

But the Marcos passed a far more severe practical test. Frank was driving. Jem was barely awake but he recalls that they were travelling downhill at about 55mph. 'I can remember a huge great pothole appearing in front of us. "Good heavens!" I thought, "If we hit this, we'll be smashed to pieces!"
'There was no way we could avoid it - we came upon it too fast. Frank braked like crazy but we were still doing about 40mph when we made contact. The offside wheel went down, then leapt out again. The rear followed suit. Then we wiggled off the road and back on again before finally coming to a halt. We looked at one another. Frank said, "Ah, well. The structure seems to be OK." "Yep," I replied. "I reckon that's as good a test as any. OK, Frank, let's get home!"'

The marine bonded plywood monocoque construction had proved itself. Despite all the extra bodywork, they had achieved their object of making a genuine roadgoing car which was also lighter than the Lotus Six. But the car also had much greater torsional rigidity than the Six and was faster as well both in top speed (around 110mph) and in 0 to 60 acceleration.
'The only problem,' explains Jem, 'was simply the time it would take to make each car because so much of it had to be hand crafted and carved. This was where Peter Adams's talents were to prove so important - in making the concept viable for small series production.'

***The prototype competes in the Six Hour Relay Race at Silverstone. Lotus 6s and 7s make up the rest of the team. Note that an oil overheating problem has now been cured by fitting a cooler above the nose cone***

The chassis for the second Marcos had already been laid down in the old coach house behind the Golden Lion Hotel by the time the new workshop being built by Frank's father was finished. From then on, work speeded up dramatically and there was even room to build two cars.

The financial position of Speedex was worsening due to a changing market and Jem had to base himself at Luton to drum up sales for the new car. The first buyer was Bill Moss, the son of a Luton garage proprietor and a driver who was already making a name for himself in an ERA. He dropped in one day to have a chat, happened to see the prototype and claimed to actually like it, which Jem found difficult to believe. But he proved it by insisting on buying the second model on the spot, even though it was still unfinished.

There was only one problem, Jem explained. Marcos would receive much more publicity if the car was entered in the GT racing category. The added advantage was that, although the publicity was greater, the competition was actually less than in the closely contested 1172 Formula, being mainly hotted-up Austin-Healey Sprites. The downside, said Jem, was that the engine he wanted was a 1-litre Keith Duckworth-tuned Ford which cost a great deal more than an 1172 unit and, unfortunately, he was experiencing a temporary cash flow problem.........

To his great relief, Bill suggested that, if he bought the engine, would Jem install and maintain the car throughout the 1960 season? The problem was resolved.

The reason Jem chose the Duckworth Ford engine is interesting. He had originally planned to use the BMC unit (as used in the Sprites) and beat them at their own game by installing it in a better chassis. 'But,' as he says, 'I happened to pop in to see Keith Duckworth who, at that time, was working in a shed, and I noticed that his engine had eight holes [ports] in the cylinder head. I figured that this must make it more efficient than the five holes [two inlet and three exhaust] of the BMC engine.'

How right he proved to be. Keith Duckworth was in partnership with Frank Costin's brother Mike, and they were later to be made famous by the 3-litre Ford Cosworth V8 engines which Lotus used to revolutionise Grand Prix racing in 1967. Ford Cosworth units have been used ever since; as late as 1994, Michael Schumacher's Benetton car used one to win the World

Championship. The Costin family has thus left its name in two famous motoring enterprises.

The only real styling difference between the second, Bill Moss, car and the prototype was that the cycle-type front wings were replaced by a Frank Costin designed all-enveloping nose which actually made the car significantly wider at the front than the rear. This seems to have been largely reaction to a comment in an Australian motoring magazine which sarcastically named the car, 'the flying splinter'. Call your own baby ugly if you want, but don't let anyone else do it. Jem just dismissed the change as, 'hideously ugly.' Dennis was more articulate: 'With a big, bulging nose for bandaged toes, a narrowing rear body for the heel and a near vertical windscreen and stubby roof section for the ankle, it was definitely a club foot! Most offensive from a sculptural point of view.' The car was, however, more familiarly known as either the Ugly Duckling or the Wooden Wonder, depending on whether you were a fan or not.

Bill Moss's first time out with the car was at a Saturday meeting at Oulton Park. It was an auspicious occasion. Even though the car was untried and completely untested, he set the fastest lap times in practice with no effort at all, but never got to race. He had used standard road plugs to drive the car to the circuit but, unfortunately, these were not changed for the race and the result was a burnt-out piston.
Bill was also due at Brands Hatch on the Sunday, so, while Jem set off for Cosworth in London to pick up a set of new pistons, Bill used the Speedex VW van to tow the Marcos back to Luton, using some old string as a tow rope.
By the time Jem got back to base, Bill already had the engine stripped down. The rebuild was completed by 1.00am and, at six, they set off for Brands Hatch. Jem takes up the story of an extraordinary day which turned out to be a baptism of fire for the new model: 'Oulton Park having been a fiasco, we were entered for our first full race against all the fastest Sprites in the country, as well as some very quick GSM Deltas. We couldn't get to the circuit in time for official practice so Bill had to start from the back of the grid. At least he had no difficulty seeing the opposition. Well, it was quite incredible! He just shot right through the field - he overtook the lot of them!

At one point, at Clearways, he blasted straight round the outside of no fewer than three cars! Even John Bolster, the commentator, was having hysterics; he kept jumping up and down, repeating himself and shouting: "Look! Just look at that way that Marcos is going!" I'd never seen him so excited!'

Ugly duckling or not, that car, the first from the Marcos stable, was a winner just as Jem's own previous cars had been - only this time the winning was in much more spectacular style. The Ford Cosworth engine combined absolute reliability with speed. Giving 74bhp, it could push the car up to 118mph, unbelievably fast for a 1-litre. This, allied to control and road holding which set entirely new standards for the class, helped Bill to chalk up five lap records and 10 wins in a row: Snetterton (four times), twice each at Brands Hatch and Oulton Park, and Goodwood and Silverstone.
The only car which was going to beat him was another Marcos and the first to get their orders in were John Sutton, Chris Meek, Jackie Oliver, Gordon Jones and a director of Courtaulds called Barry Filer, who bought a car to be driven by the then unknown Jackie Stewart. This car was driven by Jem to Barry's home on the edge of Glasgow. As it was in the dead of winter and there was no heater, the drive was no picnic and Jem made full use of the semi-race engine to get the unpleasant experience over as quickly as possible; but his consolation was that Barry paid for his flight back to London, Jem's first ever trip on an airliner.

The resulting rush kept the team at Dolgellau, now five people, working seven days a week round the clock, throughout the whole of 1960. It was a punishing regime. Everyone paid for their own bed and breakfast at a small hotel in the town but would eat little else all day except when kind locals took pity and brought in trays of meals. The tradition built up, however, that, just once a week, one of them would, in rotation, treat the others to fish and chips.
Proud though the Dolgellau team was about the amazing success of the car, and of the very high standards of craftsmanship used in its construction, only Frank seemed to find its styling acceptable, an attitude difficult to reconcile with the previous works of art with which he had been associated - Lotus, Vanwall and the Lister Jaguar.

***Jackie Stewart shows a Jaguar 'E' Type the way in his first race***
(Courtesy Graham Gauld)

***Jackie Stewart on the Rest And be Thankful Hill Climb, 1961***
(Courtesy Graham Gauld)

*Stewart is reunited with his first car in 1991, after 30 years apart. Jem's daughter, Lucinda, looks bemused at this moment of history*

*In 1990, Frank Costin, aged 70, visited Silverstone, where he saw again the ex-Jackie Stewart car which had originally been designed by him*

| First place in 1,000 c.c. G.T. class | Driver | Fastest lap min. sec. |
|---|---|---|
| June 1960 Brands Hatch (old circuit) | Bill Moss | 1 6 |
| June 1960 Snetterton | Bill Moss | 2 2 |
| June 1960 Snetterton | Bill Moss | 2 1 |
| July 1960 Goodwood | Bill Moss | 1 50 |
| July 1960 Oulton Park | Bill Moss | 2 9 |
| July 1960 Snetterton | Bill Moss | 2 2 |
| July 1960 Snetterton | Bill Moss | 2 2 |
| Aug. 1960 Oulton Park | Bill Moss | 2 9 |
| Aug. 1960 Brands Hatch (new circuit) | Bill Moss | 2 4.4 |
| Aug. 1960 Silverstone | Bill Moss | 1 18 |
| Sept. 1960 Snetterton | S. Diggory | 2 3 |
| Sept. 1960 Snetterton | Chris Meek | 2 0 |

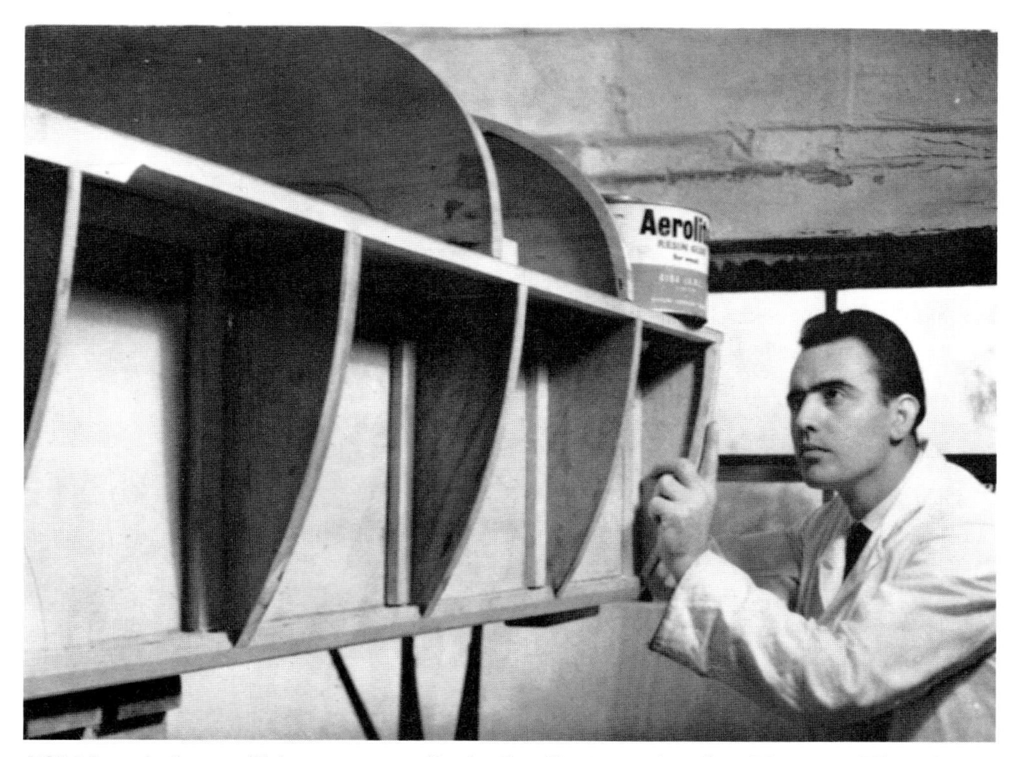


***Bill Moss's incredible race results in the first production Marcos. The photo underneath shows Dennis Adams inspecting a torque box at Dolgellau. Note the Aerolite glue, developed for use in Mosquito fighter aircraft, and used by Marcos***

Was his defence of this first Marcos obstinacy, defensiveness or an indication of a change in aesthetic values? It is hard to say but, one day, Dennis had had enough: 'Frank had gone down to Luton to see Jem for a few days,' he says. 'So I said to the boys, "I don't give a sod - I'm going to alter the bugger!"

'My plan was to change just a tiny bit on each car as we made it - a bit down the back here, a bit off the top there, lift the tail a fraction - and so on, so that Frank wouldn't notice but we could slowly get the car looking a bit better. Well, we didn't get very far. As soon as he came back, Frank spotted our change in the roof line. It was only a difference of ¾" but it was enough - he spotted it! *And* he made us change the whole thing back again!'

***Dennis Adams' original drawing shows how just small was the alteration to the roof line which was spotted by Frank Costin***

●~~~●~~~●

Although the team became well known and welcome figures in Dolgellau, Jem was unknown. It was understood locally that the finance for the project was being supplied by a Mr Marsh, a businessman from far off Luton and, from that, the assumption grew that he must therefore be a wealthy industrialist. There was therefore some excitement when it was heard that the great man would be visiting the area for a few days' holiday. Speculation abounded as to what luxury car he would arrive in. Some thought it might be a Rover. Others felt that it could be nothing less than a Bentley. They were all wrong. Jem's credibility, built over many months, was destroyed in seconds when a tiny little Austin Seven festooned with luggage like some Giles cartoon, came bounding down the road and out stepped Jem. Worse was to come when out from the tiny interior crawled his whole family.

Back home, Jem was involved in his third road accident. Tiredness due to overwork was a continuous problem for everyone in MBC and there is no doubt that is what caused the accident.
'I was driving our old Thames Ford van from home to work,' he explains, 'and was having trouble keeping my eyes open. I drove round this corner and - crash! - straight into the front of a Ford Prefect.' When the policeman asked for his statement, Jem, with great presence of mind, said that he ought not to make one for a couple of days until he tried to sort out what had happened.
'When the van was returned to Luton as a near write-off, I found that the driver's seat was loose so, when the policeman appeared, I got him to sit on it. "You sit there and turn the wheel," I said to him. He did - and fell off! "That was it!" I exclaimed. "That was what happened! You see, the seat mounting broke on me!"'

●~~~●~~~●

By the end of 1960, the strain at Dolgellau was beginning to tell. The relationship between Dennis and Frank was not helped by Frank introducing his own design work during company time: an action made even harder for Dennis and Peter to bear when they were putting in an enormous effort. In fact, they both had to spend time in bed suffering from sheer exhaustion and Dennis had lost almost three stones in weight.

Dennis was now becoming involved in working on an improved version of the Marcos to be launched at the 1961 Racing Car Show. That Frank allowed this at all showed how much he had lost interest and this was reinforced when he let Dennis and Peter make what changes they wanted to his previously fiercely protected design.

All the extra business meant that the workshop was no longer adequate so, late that year, the MBC team moved to new premises just north of Llanberis, in a prefabricated building which had been put up in the war to act as the canteen of a now disused school. This move was charmingly described, with splendid Welsh poetry, in a local newspaper: 'NEW FACTORY STARTS IN CLASSROOM. Tucked away in an old school building in Brynrefail are five young men *with a song in their hearts and skill in their fingers*' [my italics]. Despite this Welsh lyricism, only two Marcos cars were made here: both to the redesign by Dennis and which became known as the Intermediate Gullwings or, more familiarly, the Smoother Lookers or the Llanberis Smoothies. The most obvious change was a six inch increase in width back from the front wheels. This brought the whole body envelope outboard of the wheels and got rid of the club foot look. Dennis then brought the prominent rear light clusters flush with the bodywork and angled the roof line lower towards the rear, rather than heading off into space. He also tidied up the mountings for the four piece windscreen. One of these cars was fitted with a Coventry Climax engine and went to Gordon Jones.

Only six Early and two Intermediate Gullwings were made but they were enough to establish the name of Marcos on the motor racing scene. Amazingly, four are still in existence, proof of the incredible durability for which Marcos was later to become famous. One, the ex-Jackie Stewart car, is still raced by Jem. In it, he has won three Historic car championships outright. Gordon Jones's went to Japan in 1993; the John Sutton car is now in California and the 1172cc prototype is still in England with its roof chopped off.

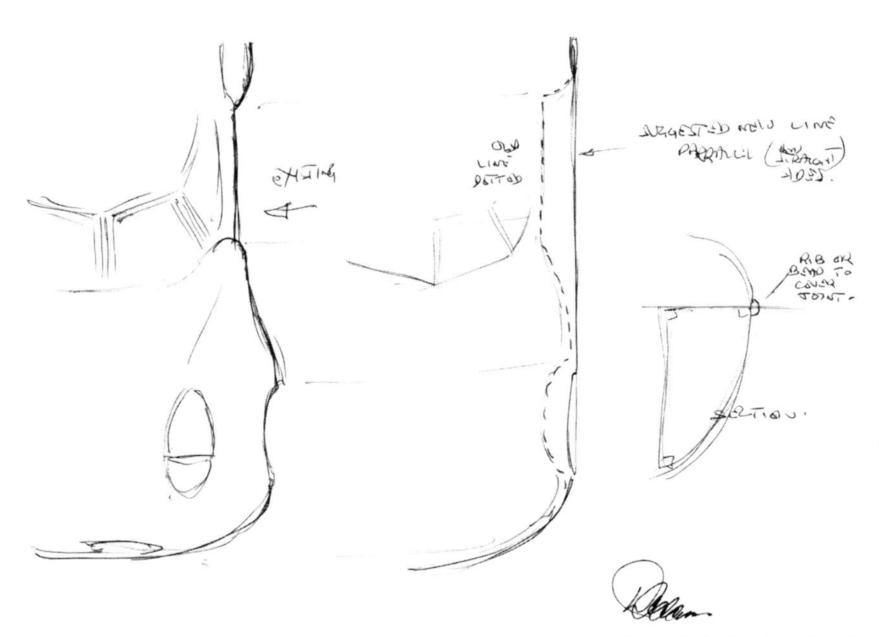


***Dennis's drawing, showing how he overcame the club foot effect***

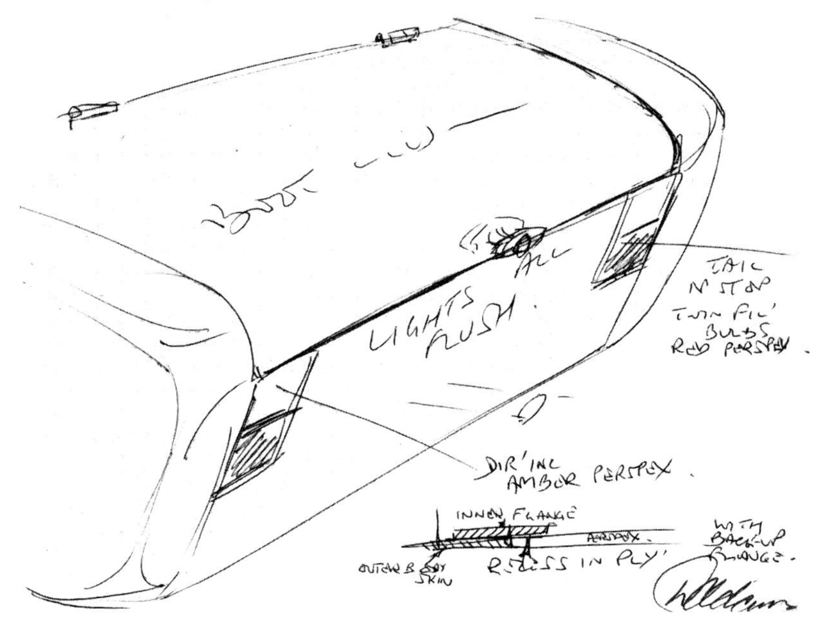


***The flush fitting rear light clusters of the Adams' design***

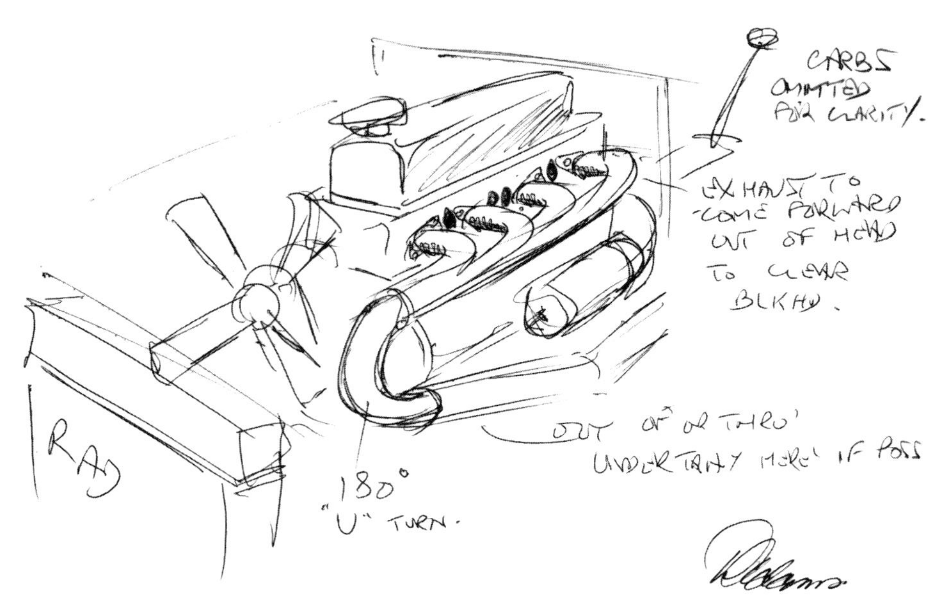


***The early cars had a unique, forward facing exhaust***

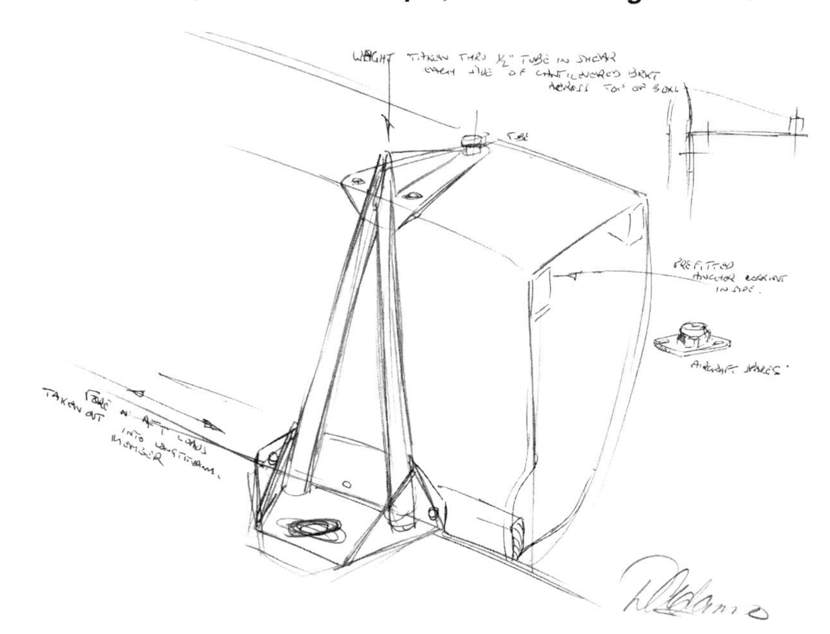


***Dennis's drawing for the engine mounting shows how the engine was hung on wooden torque boxes***

•~~~•~~~•

With the split from Frank, the Dolgellau operation was closed down and the Adams brothers moved to Luton to continue operations. If the area was more industrialised than Dolgellau, this did not mean an improvement in working conditions. As Dennis recalls: 'The workshop was a two storey house which had had the downstairs converted into a hat factory with a hole in one wall which used to be the front door, and cobbles which went round the back. We had to knock together the upstairs bedrooms to do the glassfibre work in.'

For the 1961 season, Dennis designed a new fibreglass body for the existing wooden body/chassis unit, showing the first signs of beauty of form which was later to become his, and the Marcos, hallmark. From hereon, the bodyshells of all future Marcos models were to be moulded from fibreglass. This car proved to be popular with competition drivers and 13 were produced over the next 18 months with a choice of 997cc 105E, 1340cc 109E and 1498cc 116E Ford engines.

Their work on the Gullwing now successfully completed, the Adams brothers decided to return to their home in Cambridge to do some design work on their own. Dennis and Jem's relationship is an interesting one. Although Dennis's contribution runs like a continuous band throughout the Marcos story, he and Peter, the brothers ever together, move in and out of the chronicle like characters in a play, sometimes on stage, sometimes not, but with an impact, like those of good leading actors, ever present. This informal arrangement seems to suit both Jem and Dennis perfectly. They are both strong characters, Dennis more outwardly, Jem more inwardly and with the greater resilience. Although they have both worked closely, harmoniously and intensively together when they both saw the need, it is difficult to see how they could have done so on a continuous basis without cramping each other's style. Only a loose relationship would have allowed each what they needed - the freedom to be themselves. It is doubtful if Dennis's artistic genius could have had the room to flower in any other way and there is no doubt that Marcos, the motor car industry and those many people who appreciate sheer beauty of design have been the beneficiaries.

***The wooden chassis for the Luton Gullwings were made by Walter Lawrence of Sawbridgeworth, the company which assembled Mosquitoes in World War II***

●~~~●~~~●

On the circuits in the 1961 season, Marcos cars capitalised on Bill Moss's successes of the previous year by finishing up with more than 20 first places and, in the hands of John Sutton, won the *Autosport* 1000cc Production GT Championship. Team Marcos, consisting of John Sutton, Jack Gates and John Mitchell, also won the team prize. The Marcos car was also declared the outright *Autosport* championship winner.

Unfortunately, the following year saw Speedex Castings and Accessories Limited close down as the market for special building finally collapsed. (The name was subsequently used by Speedex Autospares Limited which traded

very successfully as a mail order company, and was sold eventually to Europa Spares).
Jem had put up a tremendous battle to keep the company going until MBC could take over as a viable alternative but time finally ran out. Without such limited support as Speedex had been able to give, MBC, too, had to go.

**"AUTOSPORT" SPRINT TROPHY**

(Courtesy *Autosport*)

# CHAPTER 5

# COMMANDER GREVILLE CAVENDISH, RN (RETIRED)

Although MBC was down, as far as Jem was concerned, it was not out. A way would be found to resurrect the company but, in the meantime, he needed a job. LMB Components, another specialist constructor, was looking for someone to develop its new car, the Debonair, and Jem must have seemed like a gift from heaven. His new employer was based in Guildford, so he decided to move into rented accommodation there, selling his bungalow in Luton in the process.

In the meantime, Dennis, without the constraints of a brief to work to, was giving his imagination full rein on a revolutionary new car, the Experimental Prototype or XP. Jem was a frequent visitor to the Adams's household in Cambridge and, even at this early stage in its development, he began to get interested in its potential.

Back at LMB, the Debonair project was running into trouble. Although Jem tried to do something with the car, it was, as he says, 'far too heavy, far too expensive to produce and therefore uneconomical to build. The company had even undertaken to machine its own brake drums, rather than use mass produced components. After we had made only four cars, I persuaded the directors to cut their losses and scrap the project.'

•~~~•~~~•

With consummate timing, Lieutenant Commander Greville Cavendish, RN, appeared on the scene. Greville is an extremely likeable character - friendly, honest and straightforward. He had a passion for cars and the Marcos Owners Club has managed to catalogue some he owned during his time with the company: one, a Jensen 541, was fitted with a variety of engines which were so potent that Greville kept ruining the running gear. The most powerful of these was an Aston Martin Le Mans engine which stripped the spokes off the wheels; a Jaguar 'E' Type; Mark IX and X Jaguars; two pre-war Mercedes sports roadsters; a Morgan three-wheeler; a Pontiac Parisienne (which was used by Dennis as his wedding car); and two Fairthorpes. He was also building a special based on big BMC components, an Oldsmobile V8 engine with automatic transmission (a rarity in the UK at that time) and Rolls-Royce wheels. When this project was shelved, the parts were used as reinforcements under the floor of his garage in Freshford; so that floor has some rare collectibles cemented into it!

Jem's attraction to Greville was that he wanted to get involved with something powerful and interesting. The Marcos, a car with a history of proven success, fitted the bill exactly. Jem met him and found him to be charming, accommodating to work with and intrigued by the possibilities of getting the Gullwing back into production. His passion for cars was such that he also later invested in another specialist company, Falcon Cars which, with its 515, offered the most luxurious component car specification then available. After Greville's time, this mantle was assumed by Marcos.

It was important that Greville should meet Dennis so Jem took him up to Cambridge to do so. This was the first time that Jem had seen the XP in anything like finished form and he remembers that meeting well: 'Dennis was waving his arms everywhere over this astounding shape and Greville immediately went wildly enthusiastic. I was absolutely amazed. The XP was way ahead of its time - it was unbelievable! It was really far too futuristic but we were so excited we immediately started looking at how we could make it practical to manufacture - without any thought as to whether we could actually sell it!'

Based on the Gullwing's wooden chassis, the XP had an 'outer space' shape, like an elongated flying saucer, with a perspex bubble top. The two doors slid backwards to reveal a central driver's position flanked by a passenger seat on each side; a design which predated McLaren's production F1 GT by 31 years. Dennis incorporated an aerofoil over the top and a spoiler at the rear - possibly the first person ever to do so. It was also one of the first mid-engined designs seen in the UK, intended to take the flat six air-cooled 2.5-litre Chevrolet Corvair unit.

The decision was made. Marcos Cars Limited was formed (the first time Marcos had appeared in the company name) and the Adams brothers were taken on to continue development work on the XP while a search was started in Wiltshire (near Greville's home) for premises to recommence production of the Gullwing.

Given that Frank Costin had played no part in the story since the completion of the first Ugly Duckling, it is interesting that his name was kept incorporated in the new name. Jem says this was because the name Marcos was already established as a racing success and it was a good name that people remembered, so there was no point in changing it. But it is fitting it was kept anyway because, despite the unappealing design of the first Gullwing, it was an incredibly successful racing machine which set the tone of the company's later successes. In addition, Frank's wooden chassis was a genuine innovation which was to become the Marcos hallmark, the feature which set Marcos apart from the rest and gave it its character. Although the last wooden chassis was made in 1969 (all the ones after that first Ugly Duckling being designed by Dennis and Peter), it is still remembered today as *the* Marcos trait and, indeed, many people erroneously believe it is still used.

The name is not so inappropriate today because most people, if asked, would think it was a derivation of Marsh Company - with an 's' stuck on the end for good measure.

There is only one problem with the name Marcos. It is bad enough that ex-president Marcos of the Philippines happened to share it; worse is that his wife Imelda was notorious for the several hundred pairs of shoes she had, leading to the standard joke: 'How many pairs of shoes can you get into a Marcos boot?' For some reason, Marcos owners don't get the joke; and, if you really want to buy a Marcos, don't ask Jem that riddle........

One of Jem's faults is a grasshopper mind and talk of 'boots' led him onto another of his endless stories. 'I once went skiing,' he sidetracks, 'with Emma Zuber, a girlfriend who insisted on taking three pairs of high thigh leather boots with us around the Swiss mountains. The boot of the Marcos was rather small so parts of these boots could be seen hanging out wherever we went. But it can't have been that bad because Emma finished up owning two Marcos cars!'

Until premises for the new company were found, Paddy Gaston, who lived in Kingston-upon-Thames and was an old racing friend of Jem's, came to the rescue. Paddy developed and raced Austin-Healey Sprites with BMC works support and he offered Marcos an old wooden and corrugated shed by a railway embankment, in a disused area behind a service station of his. In this, the fledgling company stored the parts transferred from MBC and also continued development work on the XP.

***Peter and Dennis Adams with the XP jig. Peter is leaning against his own Gullwing with the top chopped off. This later became the prototype Spyder***
(Courtesy D.I. Tuddenham)

The next stage of the XP was to get a prototype aluminium body built and this was entrusted to Len and Roy Hartin of Hanwell, West London. The team could hardly have chosen better. The Hartins had a wealth of experience in aluminium body shaping going back to before the War, when they had worked on Rolls-Royces and Railtons.

Their real skills, developed during the war in the job of shaping intricate skins for fighter aircraft, gave them a feel for aerodynamics as well as delicate design. Postwar, after a short spell back in traditional coachbuilding, they fell into a ready market for racing car bodies. They made the shell for the first Cooper Formula 2 car in 1950 - and a whole plethora of Coopers after that. After the XP came prototypes for the Indianapolis Lotus, the BRP monocoque, the Formula 1 Brabham and many other sports, racing and road cars.

***A rare photo of the XP, outside the Hartins' workshop. The parked Austin A60 shows how advanced the design was for the time***

In order to make the XP palatable to the general public, it was decided to tone down the design. 'Even so,' says Dennis, 'the driver's legs went down actually between the front wheels, so we had to get the suspension and steering out of the way. We did this by designing king posts with steering arms that angled upwards to get the rack over the driver's legs. It was only later that designers of Grand Prix and GT cars came up with the same solution.'

The development work on what was to become the first Spyder, the name given to the open-topped two-seater version, was also done in that shed at Kingston. The idea came from Peter, who cut the top off his own Gullwing and the team liked what they saw. As there was no other complete car available at the time, Peter's became the development prototype.

●~~~●~~~●

In the meantime, Greville thought he had found suitable premises in Bath. He took the whole team down to have a look but, says Jem, 'He reckoned without Dennis! Dennis took one look and said, "It's bloody awful! No! I could not possibly work here!" So we drove around the area, looked at a few corrugated iron sheds, all of which met with the same response from Dennis.'
'But,' Dennis takes up the story, 'it all changed when we got to Bradford-on-Avon. As we got to the town centre, there before us was the River Avon looking very beautiful against a backdrop of cottages and the hill rising up behind them. I turned to Pete and exclaimed, "This is it! It has just got to be here - this is terrific!" We hadn't found any suitable premises, mind you, but the weir, the trees, the whole feeling of romanticism of the place - oh, it was great!'

The new Marcos works was to be in the old Royal Enfield motorcycle factory, left vacant when the company moved its operation to Westwood, just outside Bradford-on-Avon.
This building was one of great character and charm, having been converted from an old woollen mill called Greenland Mills. This choice was a happy one because, not only was Royal Enfield one of the great names in British motorcycle manufacture, but its engine had been used to power another

specialist car, a short-lived but tremendously exciting little machine called a Berkeley which bore some resemblance to a tiny Marcos and which, in its day was a also a giant killer. Powered by only a 750cc Super Constellation engine, it regularly trounced much bigger-engined Sprites, the same competition against which the first Marcos Gullwing had so successfully cut its teeth.

All in all, 1962 was proving to be an eventful year, matched by Marcos successes on the track. Although Jem had neither the time nor the money to indulge in his hobby, the company did prepare cars for willing customers who, between them, consolidated the Marcos reputation as a race winner. Tommy Weber was overall winner of the French AGAC Coupe de Paris held at Montlhéry, in his 997cc car. Apart from a class win in the International Trophy race at Silverstone, Steve Minoprio won 20 races and broke seven lap records on his way to taking the *Autosport* 1000cc GT Championship, the second year in a row for Marcos. He, Grahame John and David Rees again won the team prize, taking 20 first places in the process. The total tally of Marcos successes in 1961 to 1962 appears to be in excess of a staggering 40 outright wins! This prompted *Autosport*, early in 1963, to describe the Gullwing as, 'a formidable racing car.'

***Gordon Jones also had a successful 1962 season in his Climax-engined Gullwing***

The move to Bradford-on-Avon was not completed until December 1962, during one of the worst winters in living memory. When Dennis and Peter Adams arrived with the removal lorries, they found the snow too deep to get through to the new works. So the brothers set to and dug a track fully 750 yards long to reach it. It took them five hours and then, painfully, everything had to be manhandled. The whole exercise took a day and a half in freezing conditions.

Although this workshop was better than anything Jem had yet had - a level concrete floor to work on was a luxury and there was plenty of room to spread out - it was bitterly cold. Being the ground floor of an old six storey mill with, naturally, no inter-floor insulation, the heat that was generated disappeared straight into the upper floors. A worse problem became apparent immediately the ancient coal-burning boiler for the heating was fired up: the heating pipes carrying the hot water ran, not at ground level round the walls, but along the ceiling! Not even the boiler itself was any help; it was in an outhouse.

***Greenland Mills, Bradford-on-Avon, home of Marcos from 1962 to 1969. Sadly, this burnt down in January 1995, just before publication of this book***

As soon as the move was completed, the immediate need was to get a car ready for the London Racing Car Show in January, so that the company could draw in some much needed cash from sales. Although the XP had come back from Hartins with its new aluminium body shell, it was nowhere near ready to show so Jem made the decision go with the Spyder. Sales from this would allow them to complete cars with the minimum of investment, from the remains of the Luton spares.

The Spyder was the first Marcos to be trimmed with an eye to comfort. With its fitted luxury carpets, used even to line the boot, it was the first component car to genuinely compare in finish with production models and, indeed, was far better appointed than many of those. Sumptuous interior trimming was a feature which Jem was to retain on all the later models and it has favourably impressed many motoring journalists throughout the years; as *Alternative Cars* put it: 'The cockpit bears comparison with virtually any exotic car that one might care to name.'

Despite this, the Spyder was not well received at the Show, the general consensus being that it needed a hard-top. In other words, Marcos had gone down a blind alley. The real crowd-puller was Eric Broadley's V8 powered Lola GT, later to be taken over by Ford as the famous GT40. Already put on the back-burner by the company's need to get immediate sales, the success of the Lola made Jem question whether the XP did have a future. Anyway, the answer was academic - Marcos needed sales now and the quickest way Jem could see of achieving this was to put the top back onto the Spyder. Dennis was not in agreement with this. Apart from anything else, with a hard-top fitted, the car doors would be tiny. Jem insisted.

'In a fit of rage,' Dennis remembers, 'I grabbed a great lump of foam, dumped it on top of the Spyder and hacked it into shape with a giant breadknife. "Right!" I shouted, "You've got what you wanted!" And everyone thought the blasted thing was beautiful - they loved it!' Thus died the Spyder (it was to be relaunched in 1985) and so was born the Marcos Fastback.

The first three Fastbacks were actually Spyders supplied with detachable hard-tops. This was not popular and it is believed that all three had their hard-tops bonded on permanently. Thereafter, in the main, the company fitted the hard-top as integral to the construction, although three subsequent cars (including that raced by Derek Bell, the future five times Le Mans winner, for E.W. Cuff Miller) are known to have had detachable hard-tops.

Perhaps the most amusing incident which occurred at the works did not concern a Marcos employee at all, but a pleasant young man who worked at the printers next door. He took to parking his three-wheeler Reliant car on Marcos property, on one occasion choosing to nose up against a 12 foot high, free-standing solid stone pillar. Later in the day, he was directing an articulated lorry backwards from the printing works and, forgetting about the presence of the pillar (and, more to the point, his car behind it), sent the lorry straight into it. The pillar was no match for the lorry; it fell over and several tons of stone completely flattened the poor Reliant. All that could be seen of it afterwards were a few strands of fibreglass spreading out from underneath the pillar.

●~~~●~~~●

The Fastback was the most beautiful Marcos to date. Being developed from the Gullwing, it also had a choice of Ford engines, the 997cc 105E, 1148cc 105E, 1498cc 116E and 1650cc 116E. The shape of the Fastback gave this model a very large boot and very similar rear-end shape to the Ferrari 250 GT 'Breadvan' and it got the company one step closer to producing what it really needed: a car which people would see as a genuine road vehicle. But it had several drawbacks for everyday use: it was far too noisy and bumpy to be acceptable to the general public and, worst of all, because the chassis had retained the high Gullwing sills, the doors were too small. That did not matter in a car with an upward opening-door or in an open car like the Spyder, but it did in a hard-top with a standard door.

The Gullwing itself still sold well enough for the company to make up another four from the remaining Luton parts but the bulk of the year's sales came from the 18 Fastbacks which were sold, almost all to circuit racing customers. The company was busier than ever and, with seven employees in the workshop, bigger than it had ever been.

***The Marcos Fastback, introduced in 1963***

Jem returned to active motor sport in 1963, although still not in his own car. A friend, James Mortimer, had bought a Fastback for racing but found he preferred to participate in ways other than driving. 'So,' as Jem relates, 'we agreed that I would drive his car, sharing the expenses, while he simply enjoyed all the dramas and excitement of being involved.' It was an excellent arrangement for both of them and Jem immediately began winning. The car was a stunning sight on the track, with its special aerodynamic nose in aluminium and its silver and black livery. This car had an 1100cc Ted Martin-developed engine with dry sump lubrication giving 85bhp and a top speed of 120mph, enough to ensure that it was the quickest car in its class over the season. Even so, Jem was older than the average racing driver and had to rely on experience rather than pure skill to win races.

***Greville Cavendish, Jem and Dennis Adams and Fastback at Greenland Mills, 1963***
(Courtesy *Bath Chronicle & Herald*)

Several other Marcos raced that season with great success: Chris McLaren came second in class in the International *Daily Express* Trophy race at Silverstone; Jackie Oliver (later to race in Formula 1, and now head of the Arrows Formula 1 team), scored a class win in his Gullwing at the Martini International Trophy race, again at Silverstone. But perhaps the year's most notable Marcos driver was Tommy Weber in his Ugly Duckling, although even he had the occasional mishap; at Goodwood, in a Fastback, he broke the lap record by an amazing three seconds and was leading easily until a wheel came off - fortunately without injury to him and little to the car. Tommy claimed the distinction of being the first driver to get round the Brands Hatch short course in 60 seconds. On the Continent, the Fiat Abarths were all-conquering but Tommy managed to get among them with a second place in the 1000cc class of a sportscar race supporting the German Grand Prix. His Ugly Duckling was subsequently written off in a race accident, possibly being driven by Nicky Byrnes.

***Marcos were very popular abroad. A gullwing competes at the Course Nationaz de Côté St. Ursanne-les Rangiers in Switzerland, 1963***
(Courtesy Presse Diffusion Lausanne)

John Sutton and John Miles also took second place to an Abarth in the 1000cc class at the Nürburgring 500kms, a result described by Brian Bennett in *Autosport* as 'one of Britain's best showings ever against the might of Abarth.' In fact, it is probably more impressive that they beat a lot of very exotic machinery to come fifth overall.
So dominant were Marcos becoming on the track that *Small Car* described them as 'all-conquering' and said of a test drive of the car that it 'gave us one of the most exciting mornings at the wheel we can remember.'

Jem's competitive instinct came out early that season: 'We were all surprised to see that rear engined cars were to be allowed into the GT class. Immediately, some clever Charlie had to fit a hard top onto a Lotus 23B which was a pure racer and not a GT at all in the real sense and spirit of the regulations. I came up against this man at Castle Combe. He shot straight into the lead of course, and I had the devil's own job trying to stay in touch. There happens to be a kink in the back straight at which I would only have to ease off slightly to take at around 110mph. He, however, would have to brake dramatically to cut his much higher approach speed and I realised that I would have more margin than he to judge it right. And so it happened, the chance came for me to nip inside him on the corner - aided by the fact that it never occurred to him that anyone could do that, so he had not kept an eye on his mirror. I am afraid that, to keep him behind me until the chequered flag, I had to perform certain illegal manoeuvres but I thought, "What the hell. He was breaking the spirit of the thing."'

The Lotus driver was fuming but, after the race, a succession of Jem's track competitors came into his pit to congratulate him.

The car's only drawback was that it kept catching fire. The first time was at Castle Combe. 'I was on the back straight,' explains Jem, 'when smoke appeared in the passenger footwell. There were no fire marshals on that side of the track so I decided to get back to the pits. What I did not know was that the exhaust system had become so hot that it had melted the clutch pipe and it was clutch fluid running onto the exhaust which had started the fire. The heat had also vapourised all the brake fluid so, when I tried to slow down for the pit lane, by this time feeling rather too warm for comfort, I found I had no clutch or brakes. Still doing 85, I wrenched the car into third, skated round the last bend and managed to grind to a halt on the hand brake, by the starter's rostrum. By then there were flames everywhere and I got out very sharpish. Luckily, the marshals were on the ball and they managed to put the fire out before too much damage was done.'

They discovered later that someone had retarded the ignition and this was what caused the exhaust to get so overheated.

'The next fire was in practice at Snetterton. I was again on the back straight, when I saw flames on the passenger side. I guessed that it was probably the exhaust again, this time touching the wooden chassis. The track there is very close to the perimeter fence, on just the other side of which is a garage. So I stopped the car on the grass, nipped over the fence to the garage, grabbed a couple of empty oil cans and shot into the ladies - luckily unoccupied! Having filled the cans with water and doused the fire, I scrambled back onto the circuit, made a quick stop at the pits to jam a piece of asbestos between the exhaust and the woodwork, and carried on record the fastest time in practice!'

Jem then went on to win the race.

•~~~•~~~•

Although little has been said about Greville in this book, this chapter is dedicated to him because he has played a great part in the history of Marcos. Greville was the saviour of the company but then plenty of people have saved companies by putting money into them, only to become insufferable or interfering afterwards. Greville was not like that. If he is scarcely mentioned here, that is a compliment to the role he played because this is a book about day-to-day operations and he carefully kept out of those; although he was passionate about Marcos and filled with enthusiasm for its future, these were left to Jem, on the business and management side, and Dennis on the design and production side. Instead, Greville chose to be supportive, encouraging and motivating, ever mindful that the team was best left to get on with it: exactly the backing the team most needed.
Greville stayed with the company until the middle of 1966 when the future seemed assured. Having achieved what he wanted, he decided that it was time to move on and Jem found himself back in total control of the company.
The parting was a happy one and, ever since then, although they rarely correspond now, Jem has had fond and grateful memories of Commander Greville Cavendish, RN (Retired).

# CHAPTER 6

# THE MARCOS 1800 ARRIVES

Part way through 1963, sales of the Fastback suddenly slowed. Expediency forced yet another postponement of the XP and Jem and the Adamses all agreed that a stop-gap was needed, and fast, to give the company time to come up with a proper replacement (for which the XP was still in the running) for the Gullwing and the Fastback. The quickest temporary solution, it was agreed, was to design something around the existing wooden chassis and using, so far as was possible, the existing mechanical components. This was a turning point in the company and Jem remembers it well: 'Dennis came rushing in with a sketch on a scrap of paper and demanded to know what I thought of it. "That looks OK," I said. Thus encouraged, Dennis rushed back to his drawing board and nearly burst trying to get it all down! He just couldn't work fast enough. Suddenly it dawned on us that something special was on that board and we all sprang out of our lethargy. We knew then that we had a fantastic shape.'

That stop-gap design, so hurriedly produced and with no time to seek the original solution which he liked to bring to his work, was to give Dennis his reputation for brilliantly artistic innovation and the Marcos its timelessly identifiable personality: as beautiful as any other car and as fast as the best too......... In the event, the design was to hold up, improving all the time, from this model to the Mantula of 1984 and the Mantara which was launched 10 years after that.

Dennis describes the lead-up to his most successful creation in a much more matter-of-fact way: 'I said I'd do a quick stop-gap on the Luton chassis, just another body to give the car bit of a boost. So I whipped one up - and they're still selling it.'

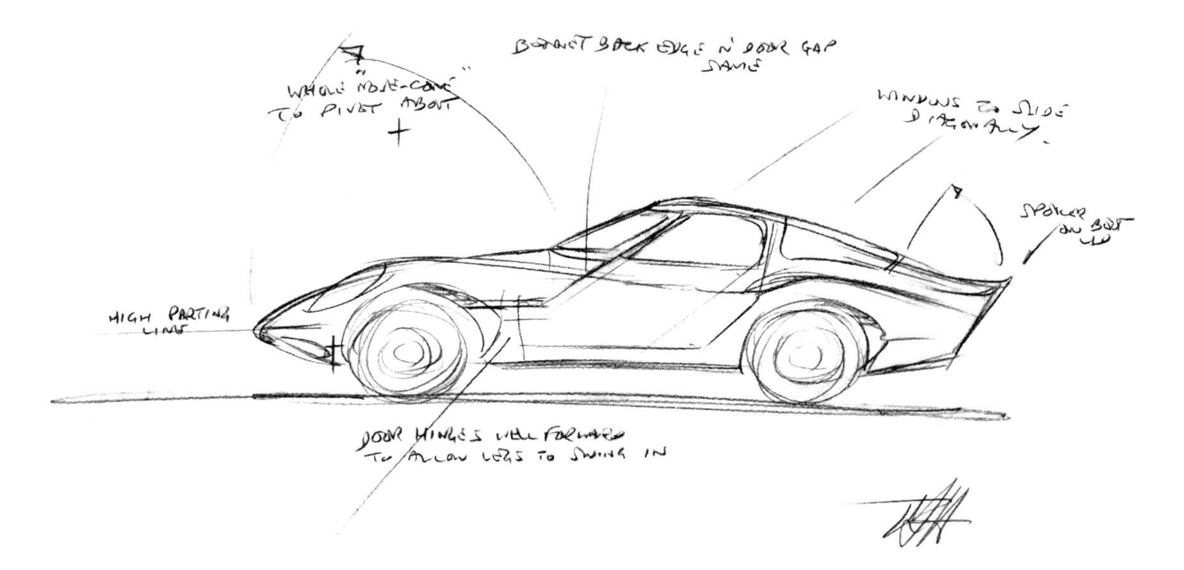


***The original drawing of what was to become the 1800, as shown by Dennis to Jem in 1963***

Dennis's taciturnity is understandable when you realise that his focus was still on the XP and when you look at how even more mind-blowing the XP would have been had it gone into production. Although I cannot see that the XP could have competed commercially with the long-term success of the new shape, there is no doubt that it would have been a clear winner if the yardstick was sheer brilliance of creativity and design, and I dare say that it is on this that Dennis would rather have been judged. As to which is more artistically beautiful, that is a matter of taste, but I doubt that the XP could have sailed unconcerned through all the changes in car fashion design over the next 31 years in the way the new Marcos was to. Nor do I believe it would have had the same universal appeal.

We will never know because, as we saw earlier, the company needed a new car urgently. The XP was not ready and this last postponement was to prove its death knell because what was to become the new car was to take up all the production energy of the works. Although, in the event, no more effort was put into the XP, it is difficult to understand why no one saw fit to save what was undoubtedly a sensational piece of work, years ahead of its time. Its components and parts were allowed to become absorbed in the junk and dust of outbuildings, pushed further and further from anyone's mind. Eventually, the aluminium body panels were left to corrode in the open before meeting their demise in a heap of rubbish. As to the chassis, no one knows what became of that. A sad end for an extraordinary vehicle. But the XP did leave two marks on history. The first is recognisable in the frontal lines of the model which was to push it to one side. The second is the badge. For the XP, Dennis had designed a suitably futuristic three-dimensional badge. He reduced this to a two dimensional one and added a red strip to the existing blue and white background for patriotic reasons, making the strip diagonal to suggest a heraldic influence; this has been the company logo ever since. I always felt that the one thing which let the car down was that badge until it was pointed out that the diagonal strip, in heraldic terms, can mean a 'bastard', an epithet no doubt frequently used by competitors on the track!

What was becoming a habitual end of year mad dash ensued as the company sought to get the new car ready for the January 1964 Racing Car Show. This time, there was an extra challenge. Jem knew that he must find a car which would not only be a potential race winner but would also appeal more to the road user than Marcos cars had so far been able to do, and this new model had to be it. This was to be the biggest launch yet of a new Marcos and, to exploit the potential of the new car, Jem felt that he needed to bring in someone to oversee the operation. His choice fell on Stan Gray. Stan and he had first met around 1950, when they were travelling in opposite directions on the Plymouth-Salcombe road. Both being in specials, Jem in his 750 and Stan in an MG Ford, they waved to each other. Coincidence decreed that they should meet up again that day, going the other way. So they stopped and a quick chat turned into an enduring friendship. Stan stayed with Jem until early 1966, then worked with Johnny Walker in Gloucester, on his attractive JWA Formula 4 racing cars, before returning to Marcos in late 1967 to oversee the XP Mantis project.

***Cut away of the 1800***

As far as racing drivers are concerned, as long as a car is a winner, they are not too concerned with the amenities provided they can, somehow, get in and out of it and actually drive it. But the general public expect greater concern for their needs and, above all, the cockpit has to be right. The Adamses decided that the easy answer was to physically build the cockpit around a model and Jem, with his height, was considered to be ideal; if he could get in, so could anyone else.
'I was stuck in the middle of the mock-up with sheets of ply everywhere,' he recalls. 'Dennis was giving me instructions like, "lean back a bit," or, "move sideways slightly," while, at the same time, Peter was trying to cut bits off here and add bits on there. Eventually, they got the position just right for me. But of course, when Dennis, with his much shorter frame, tried it, he

could not reach the pedals. "Easy," he said, "I'll just design the whole pedal assembly to move forwards and backwards."'
This movable pedal assembly was also to become a Marcos hallmark. To this day, no other car company has used the same solution, preferring to slavishly follow the harder, more expensive and less aesthetically pleasing tradition of making the seats movable.
Some time later, Jem, much to his amusement, got an irate letter from the then British Motor Corporation telling him that they had a patent on the idea of the movable pedal assembly and telling him to desist from further use immediately. 'I decided to ignore it,' he says, 'because I did not believe that the mighty BMC would act against a little company making specialist sportscars.' He was right.

***The movable pedal assembly. One of the hallmarks of the Marcos***

One result of the cockpit planning was that this car was one of the first ever to offer head restraints, for both driver and passenger. As Jem said, 'This was not just for comfort, although the semi-reclining position almost required a "pillow", but to guard against having one's neck broken in a rearward impact.' Only later was the word 'whiplash' coined and only later did this become standard even among the designers of fast cars.

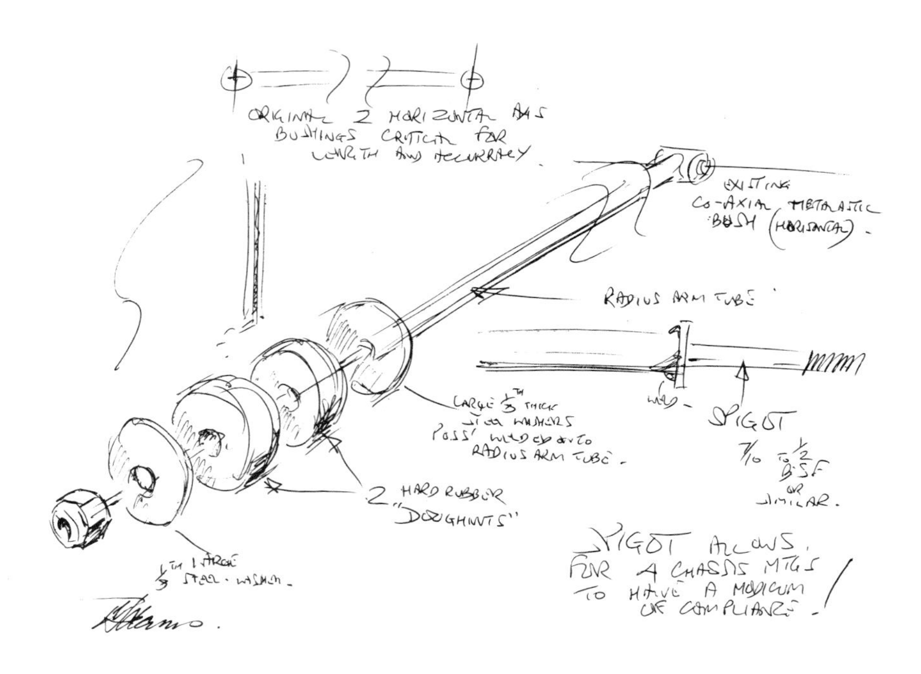


***Rear axle location showing how the radius rods were set either side of a wooden diaphragm***

Sports coupés of those days and since seem to have been designed with midgets in mind, possibly because a cockpit which would take a tall man would spoil the aesthetic lines of a designer's beloved shape. Most of them either sacrifice sales to tall drivers for the sake of retaining their clean lines (like many of the Lotuses) or, like the Jaguar 'E' Type, stick a large bobble on for the cabin. Dennis Adams proved that, to a good designer, this need not present a problem; the Marcos, despite being one of the lowest GTs around and four inches lower than the 'E' Type, is capable of taking perhaps the tallest drivers of any sportscar - up to 6'7" tall - all without spoiling the low, sleek shape. This all sounds like clever design but I prefer

Jem's explanation: 'I could not find a GT I could fit into, so I thought I had better build one for myself.'
In fact, the height of the Marcos is, along with its shape and its wooden chassis, one of its characteristic features. 'If you put a cushion under the dining room table and then try to sit on it, you will have a fair idea of Marcos dimensions' was how Geoff Le Prevost put it, writing in *Practical Classics* (February 1984). It is only 3'6½" high, reaching only an average man's belt buckle. This means that you look up to a Mini and, in fact are little taller than a lorry tyre.
As each Marcos is designed round the buyer, people of any height can be made comfortable. If anyone has a problem, it is the short occasional driver and the company later found a solution for them in a tadpole-shaped dummy seat designed to go over the existing one. The name Tadpole stuck and it worked extremely well, so well, in fact, that one car was even built to accommodate a husband of 6'4" and wife of 5'1" without any problems for either!

A new car also gave the opportunity to change the power unit. The company wanted a more upmarket image than Ford offered at that time. Ford themselves had still not started active participation in motor sport even though, at that time, almost every other specialist car company was following the path of stretching the standard Ford engines to their limits. This had given a 'boy racer' image to Ford powered machines, not what Marcos wanted. Apart from this, the team felt that it made good sense to look elsewhere for a power unit which could match the Fords at full stretch without any modification at all. Their first choice was a BMW engine but it proved too difficult to fit the slant engine and its sump. The power unit eventually chosen was the unlikely 1800cc Volvo B18 engine. Given that Volvo, with all its technology and resources, had only managed a failure with its own P1800 sportscar, the choice of this apparently incongruous and unlikely power unit was an inspired one. Jem dismisses it by saying, 'Having decided we did not want to use a Ford, this was the only engine we could find which would fit.' But how many people, given the image of Volvo and the pathetic performance of its sportscar, would have even tried it? It took Volvo until the early 1980s to come out with race-competitive machinery, when they launched their very successful turbos.

●~~~●~~~●

The reception the 1800 got at the 1964 London Racing Car Show was incredible. For once, the Marcos team was ahead of itself. As Jem says, 'We actually managed to get two cars ready - and one actually worked! Such a state of readiness was almost unheard of from a specialist in those days!'

Crowds surrounded the Marcos stand all day long. The press were ecstatic: 'the most impressive of these cars is the new Marcos 1800'; 'the "prima donna" of the Show'; 'one of the most attractive and stylish of the cars at the Show is the Marcos 1800'; 'other star attractions at the Show were the Marcos 1800 GT'; 'another star of the show is undoubtedly the Marcos 1800'; 'the star attraction at the Show'; 'the most interesting newcomer is the Marcos 1800'; 'the most exciting development since the Lola GT'; 'this year another GT car stole a lot of the limelight and rightly so'; 'the Volvo engined Marcos 1800, which undoubtedly stole the Show'.

But then the unforeseen happened: no one would buy it. In fact, the design was too successful; it was as if people felt it was too good to be true, too far ahead of its time. It was, to their collective mind, more like a concept car than the real thing. And nobody buys a concept car. But the impact on the company was not too serious. There was still plenty of work to be done to get the 1800 into production and the work force was having to be increased just to maintain the many road and competition cars which were around by then. The company was also having to take over more of Greenland Mills - all six floors of which, apart from Marcos, were empty.

Terry Sanger, a competition driver and an extrovert from the West Country, joined the company, and Jem immediately put him onto testing the 1800. To put it through its paces, Dennis and Terry took the car to Charmey Down, a very rough wartime airstrip, now disused, just north of Bath. The testing session went very much to Dennis's liking but, when he tried to call it a day, Terry decided instead to do just one more lap, this time, he said, he wanted to really give the car its head. Dennis was horrified but he was too late to stop him.

'The next moment,' Dennis relates, 'Terry came hammering towards the corner at the end of the main runway with dust, wheat ears and all sorts of rubbish swirling like a typhoon around the back of our beautiful baby. "My

God!" I thought, "He'll never make it!" And he didn't. He spun it - and it spun on, and on, and on, right off the runway, across the grass strip, and, still spinning, crashed through a fence and finished up in this cornfield. There lay our lovely car covered with corn and muck, a barbed wire fence entangled all over the bonnet and around the wipers, and with scratches everywhere. "Right!" I said. "We'll go home now - *if*, by any chance, you've finished testing?"
'We had thought we were on Air Ministry land. Unfortunately, we found out we weren't when the landowner turned up with a shotgun and padlocked the gate. He was fed up with people tearing round on his land and a great argument followed. Eventually, we managed to calm him down and he let us out.'

Media interest in the car suddenly hit a high and, for the first time, Jem experienced the joys of television interviews and the self-satisfying requests from agencies to borrow cars for exotic advertising. This was sooner or later bound to attract the social set. Natalie Goodwin, daughter of a director of the Cussons toiletries giant, wanted a car in her favourite colours of marigold and black. Jem managed to talk her out of this and she finally collected an all-black Marcos with marigold-piped upholstery. Prince Albrecht of Liechtenstein, Lord Lilford and Lord Cross all placed orders. Jem also drove one of these cars in an episode of the TV series *The Saint*. Needless to say, the car was being driven by the 'baddy', escaping from the hero, Roger Moore. In just over four years, Jem had gone from Austin Seven constructor to manufacturer of exotic GT cars.
The motoring press, too, was clamouring for test cars. Jem refused them all; the car was not yet ready to be subjected to the rigours of press drivers. But, in the end, he knew he had to do something.
'So I decided to hold a press reception with loads of booze to keep the press boys happy,' explains Jem. 'There was no way I would let them see the shambles of our workshops, so we hired a local garage for the day and, not wanting to get any dirt on the car, I arranged to have it taken over on a trailer. Well, it was a good day and about 40 press people turned up. It all went OK until they, having crawled all over it, wanted to give it a run. "No way!" I said. And it is just as well I did. After they all left, I decided to drive the car back. I hadn't gone more than a few yards when a wheel fell off!'

This had been caused by an undetected fault in the drive shaft assembly and several of the early cars lost wheels - fortunately without anyone getting hurt - before it was found and rectified.
Jem finally had to give in to press requests for a test. But he was still worried about how they would react to actually driving what was a new concept for its time. The answer, he hoped, was that, in a motoring journalist's eyes, sheer power would make them overlook anything else; so he decided to race three Marcos on the M4 motorway to see which was the fastest, then give that one to the journalists to try. It worked.

In contrast with press excitement, sales were disappointingly slow. No one else could offer a car even remotely similar and, at £1,500 for a complete car in component form, it offered real individuality at an affordable price. Fortunately, the lack of sales did not yet matter too much because it was autumn before the works were geared up to build even one car a week. This was partly due to a shortage of staff which meant that everyone had to do everyone else's job, and partly because parts could only be bought as and when they were needed.
The 1800 had been launched as a road car, so it was much to the team's surprise that all the early buyers were club racers, and the car soon proved to be as much of a race winner as the earlier models had been. But, by late 1964, the company had eliminated some of the early faults: lack of adequate heating had put off some buyers and the early models were let down by ugly, vertically sliding perspex side windows. But sales still did not improve. Was the price too high? Although it had started at £1,500, continuous refinements had pushed it up. On the grounds that this was causing sales resistance the team, after 33 cars were built, replaced the original expensive de Dion type independent rear suspension, which had been manufactured by Marcos, to a proprietary Ford live rear axle. This allowed a price reduction to £1,340, but still sales did not increase.

•~~~•~~~•

For the 1964 racing season, Jem continued to drive James Mortimer's car. Again, it proved the quickest car in its class and he finished a two year stint with another long list of wins.

James subsequently sold this car and it ended its days as it had threatened to do twice in 1963: by catching fire - this time at Snetterton circuit. Unfortunately, third time round, the marshals could do nothing to save it.
Derek Bell was also to be seen on the circuits in a Marcos, driving a 997cc Fastback owned by E.W. Cuff Miller.

Marcos cars finished first and third at the Japanese Grand Prix for GT cars, but then fell foul of politics. The story of this extraordinary race is taken up by Mike Knight, the 'winner': 'We were up against the Honda S600s but the Marcoses were very much quicker. However, Honda had to win at all costs because the Japanese could not believe that a wooden box on wheels could beat their high tech cars with their four-cam engines, so they demoted me to fifth place, first behind the Hondas. But they did allow me to keep the winner's prize money and the trophy! This is the first time I have ever heard of somebody being disqualified, yet allowed to keep the winner's spoils!'
There is a splendid account of this race meeting in a cutting from a magazine which I am unfortunately unable to identify. The event started with a race for touring cars in which the first 12 places were taken by Datsun Bluebirds. The unidentified reporter then goes on to describe the second race, for GTs: *'The racing was characterised by three competing types of car, Honda Motor's S600, Marcos GT, from Britain and Hino Motor's Contessa.*
*'A well-known Marcos GT, driven by the skilful expert driver Michael Knight, made its way up at a fast pitch and topped on the 4th lap. Though placed second on the 5th lap, Knight continued thereafter to run ahead of others to the end.*
*'Arthur Owen, driving another Marcos GT, placed third in the goal, having displayed his full strength from round the 6th lap.*
*'However, Knight was placed down to fifth, unfortunately, as he had played foul at the flying start and Arthur Owen was disqualified as his car was found out of standards. After all, Ronnie Buchnum* (sic), *driving a Honda Motor's S600 won the race.'* (Ronnie Bucknum, an American, later raced Formula 1 Hondas).

***A works team entered two Fastbacks for the Nürburgring in 1964. This is one of them, with the pit crew and 'Le Patron' (Jem) behind***

***The second of the two Works Fastbacks racing at the Nürburgring, 1964***
(Courtesy E. Jelinek)

*Speedex 750 Formula Car. Jem with his son Christopher and Bess the Jack Russell looking on. 1958.*

*Marcos 1800 Coupé – The initial classic design by Dennis Adams on which all future models have been based.*

*3 litre Ford wooden chassis Marcos fitted with Marcos Alloy wheels and sunroof, 1968.*

*Mantis 2+2 circa 1969. Fitted with 2.5 fuel injection Triumph engine.*

*The Marcos fast back, nicknamed "The Breadvan" on the way to another win at Thruxton.*

*Special High Performance Marcos Mantula built for the Japanese Market....*

*....with racing engine fitted giving exceptional performance.*

***Jem Marsh in the ex-Jackie Stewart Marcos in action at Nurburgring, Germany at "The Oldtimers" Historic Meeting. 1989.***

***Marcos XP prototype circa 1963, showing the seating design which predated the McLaren F1 GT by 30 years.***

*Jem Marsh being chased by Dave Abbott in his immaculate Gullwing Marcos.*

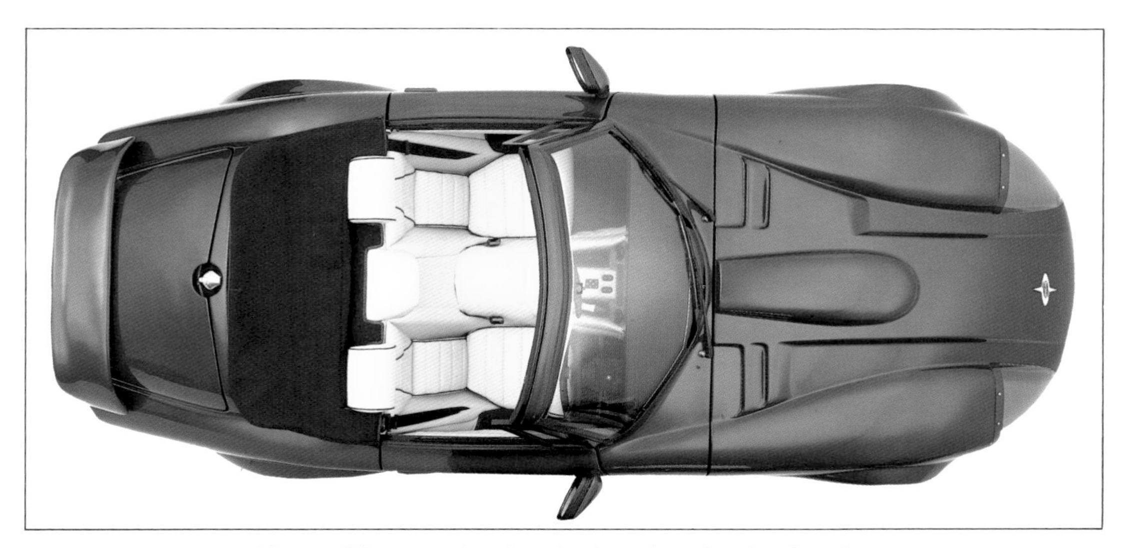

***Marcos Mantara showing the luxurious leather interior.***

***The Mantara has ample room for two sets of Golf clubs and luggage in one of the biggest boots for a two-seater sports car.***

*The first Marcos Mantula fitted with the 3.5 Rover engine, 1984.*

•~~~•~~~•

The 1800 was again used as the Marcos flagship for the 1965 Racing Car Show. Although this resulted in no dramatic change in fortunes, the motoring press, quite extraordinarily for it is under constant pressure to find something new for the public's voracious appetite and therefore tends to dismiss last year's model as 'old', the 1800 once again took its fancy with such comments as: 'Probably the most elegant car in the Show is the Marcos 1800'; 'Marcos 1800, highlight for many of Show'; An outstanding exhibit at the Show is the Marcos 1800'.
Dennis was really starting to bloom as a designer, so the company decided to stage an exhibition of his drawings and designs on the stand with the aim of promoting him as a separate entity within the Marcos empire.

Despite press support, it really took two years to get public acceptance of the 1800's shape. Although Jem was frustrated by this, Dennis was not so. 'Even had the sales been there,' he explains, 'we could not have produced any more cars. There was a lot to learn about fibreglass. For instance, just take the doors; they were always a problem to fit right. Our fitter was a Welshman with the unlikely name of Leslie Loosemore. He used to wear a butcher's apron with a large front pocket which was always full of little knobs of wood identified with little Welsh signs which no one except him understood. When a wooden chassis was ready for its fibreglass shell, he would position the body first with about thirty of these blocks put all over the place. Next, he would get the doors right. Only then would he allow the body to be laminated to the chassis, after which those blocks came out.'

•~~~•~~~•

Whether or not Marcos could have produced more cars, it did find time to diversify into such strange things as fibreglass slides for children. The determination to stay with the 1800, despite its disappointing sales, also meant that the Adams brothers were no longer fully occupied on the cars so a development section was formed to take in such varied outside work as boats, grain hoppers, a bobsleigh and even a church steeple. But the most extraordinary project of all was a commuter car designed to stand up on end to save street parking space.

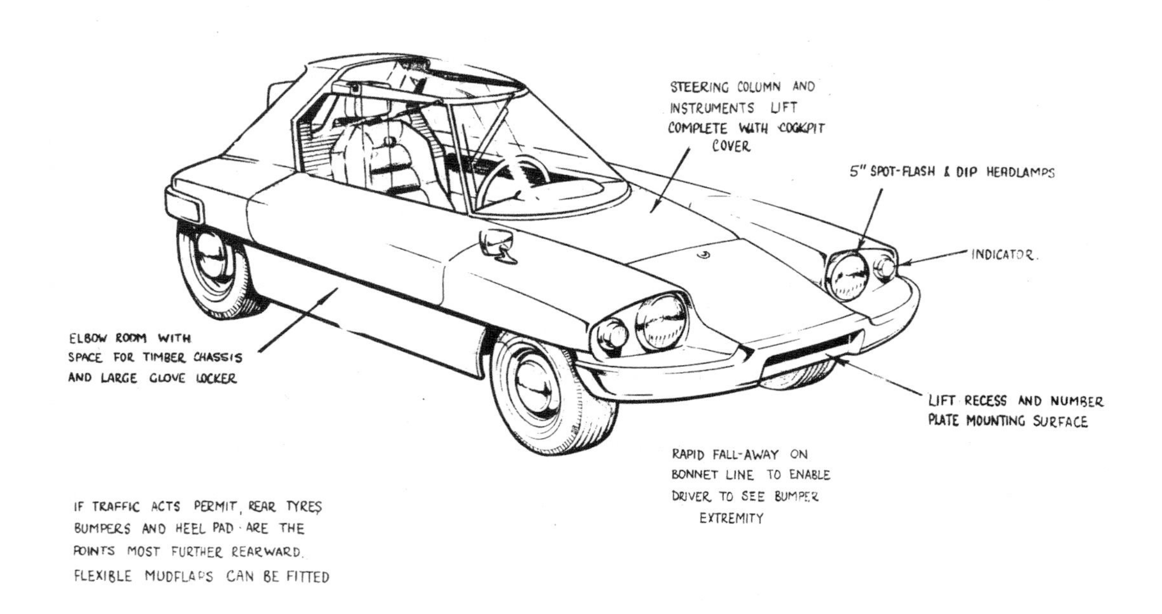


***The Commuter Car Project***

This oddity was the result of an initiative by Ernest Marples, famous as the Minister of Transport who could not drive. The project was initiated by a consortium of businessmen, one of whom was Ian Winterbottom, then Conservative MP for Nottingham Central. Dennis designed a vehicle round a 250cc motorcycle engine. Only eight feet long, it was so compact that three cars could have parked in the space of one Mini. The major problems were how to avoid fuel and battery acid spillage and how to make the car easy for one person to up-end.

Dennis found solutions to all these problems and actually came up with a workable idea but, sadly, the consortium shelved the scheme.

Some of the Adams's ideas were directly related to Marcos cars and one of Peter's projects in the development shop was one powered by a 3.5-litre V8

Buick engine. This unit was so large that it protruded right back into the cockpit, requiring a drastically shortened footwell - so short, in fact, that only Peter could drive it. This was the first Marcos to have automatic transmission but it turned out to be a hindrance rather than a help because there was so much power that even a light touch on the throttle was enough to set the rear wheels spinning.

This was a mean-tempered car, and an unhappy project. On one occasion, Peter was working under the bonnet with the engine ticking over. Unknown to him, the transmission was in drive so, when he blipped the carburettor, he had the shock of his life as the car shot forward and pinned him under a bench.

On another occasion, Peter had temporarily situated the petrol pumps in the boot. While he was working on them, he accidentally flipped their contacts; these promptly sparked and exploded the petrol fumes in the boot. Peter was sent flying backwards. Stunned and with his eyebrows singed, he staggered up and slammed the boot lid on the flames as a temporary expedient until he could find a fire extinguisher. Eventually he located one, filled the boot with foam and shut the lid again. It worked.

The project was abandoned soon afterwards. But what is interesting about this story is that the engine with which Peter experimented was the all-aluminium Buick unit later to be adopted by Rover and was the fore-runner of the one used by Marcos from 1984 onwards. No one realised it, but Peter was 19 years ahead of his time!

One of the 1800s was built to a special lightweight racing specification for Howard Faure and Morning Star Racing. Before delivering it, Jem decided to give the car a baptism of fire by entering it in the prestigious 150 mile Martini International race, at Silverstone. The entry list reads like the *Who's Who?* of racing at the time: Bruce McLaren (whose place was taken in the race by Chris Amon), John Surtees, the then reigning Formula 1 World Champion, Peter Revson, Jackie Stewart, Frank Gardner, Roy Salvadori, Jack Sears, Tommy Hitchcock, David Piper, Roy Pike, Peter Gethin, Jackie Oliver, Hugh Dibley, and Jim Clark. It is worth mentioning that, while drivers of this stature expect to have full-race prepared machinery waiting for them,

Jem had to drive his car to the circuit, yet he still managed to beat a lot of them!

•~~~•~~~•

***The woodwork shop, Greenland Mills***

Marcos was now needing more and more space. By the end of 1965, it had taken up five floors of Greenland Mills, spread out alongside to another two single storey workshops which housed the stores and the spray shop, and through another unit for stores before finishing up across the road and by the riverside, where offices, a fibreglass department, an engine development section, the Adams's drawing office and prototype and development shop were situated. This last was particularly at risk from flooding.

Staff numbers, too, had grown apace to 50 but, fortunately, getting staff was not a problem. The Avon Rubber Company was not far away and it was easy to attract people who were happy to take lower wages to work in a much more interesting and happier atmosphere. Indeed, people seemed to share a lot of after hours fun together. Dennis recollects that Terry Sanger bought, of all things, a complete fire engine. 'We often used to climb onto this thing and belt off for a jar or two.' Dennis recollects. 'In fact, it had its uses on nights out. Bath is an appalling town for parking restrictions, but not for us; if we wanted to eat out, we just parked the fire engine on the double yellow lines outside the restaurant!'

On another occasion, the works were challenged to a conker match by a team from Aust, north of Bristol. It was all highly professional, with various classes according to weight of conker and length of string, but the one which really interested the Marcos team members was the Formula Libre in which anything went.
So they set to to construct the heaviest conker they could. The carpenters who worked on the wooden chassis got a great lump of elm and bored a hole through it. This was passed to the assembly shop where eight feet of the thickest tow rope they could find was threaded through it and a monster knot was waxed at the end. From there, it went to the fibreglass department, where the wooden lump was encased in two halves of a two foot fibreglass ball made from moulds in all the right conker colours. There was some doubt as to whether this conker could be swung so it was taken outside for performance testing. It was found that, up to a critical speed, it was controllable but, if the player tried to swing it too fast, the conker would take over and he would end up spinning too, rather like a hammer thrower. The test was deemed passed.
The rest of the team, dressed in a variety of fancy dress from pyjamas to sports clothes, got to the pub ahead of the Marcos conker player, only to find themselves threatened by a gang of teddy boys who took exception to the way they were dressed. Fortunately, at that point, the conker player arrived. Whether it was his dress of rugby shorts, running vest, one cricket and one football boot, one cricket pad and one boxing glove with a rugby scrum cap on his head, or whether it was the massive size of the conker he

was wielding, the teddy boys thought better of it and went off, no doubt to find another pub to terrorise.
The massive Marcos conker should have been no match for the home team's Formula Libre entry, which was a one inch diameter hardened steel ball on a four foot braided high tensile steel wire - David and Goliath in reverse. While, with this steel ball, they could get a good swing at the Marcos conker, the Marcos player, despite having to clear the bar in order to get a swing going and looking fearsome in the process, could generate only enough momentum to push the home team's 'conker' out of the way. However, the Marcos team won by default, when no further home team player could be found willing to risk life and limb by stepping forward to meet the whirling Marcos entry.

As the year went on, the Adams brothers became increasingly involved with other activities. Although these projects were officially contracted on behalf of Marcos, a proper split became more logical and June saw the brothers leave to set up on their own. The move, in fact, was only a few yards down the road to a charming property called The Old Forge. (The Forge was to figure again in Jem's life. In 1994, Jem and Lyn turned it into Lailey's Gallery, specialising in paintings and prints, particularly those of Sir William Russell Flint. Jem has amassed 183 racing trophies to date and these are also housed here. The opening of the Gallery and Jem and Lyn's wedding took place within four weeks of each other so it seemed fitting that this should also be the unusual setting for their wedding reception.)

•~~~•~~~•

Although the 1966 Racing Car Show produced some extra sales, the boost was short-lived and Jem soon found, to his consternation, that, for the first time in the company's history, cars were being stock-piled. It seemed difficult to know where to turn next but he knew that the tide must eventually turn in his favour when Corgi Toys made a model of the Marcos 1800. He explains: 'As a car manufacturer, you know you've got a hit on your hands when Corgi make a model of your car. If they can sell the model, you can sell the real thing. In a funny sort of way, that model means more to me than even some of the great successes we have had at trade shows!'

Corgi was right because just then, as so often happens in the Marcos story, the opportune happened. This time, it was Ford's decision to get involved officially in motor sport. Its success on the race tracks led to customer demand for Ford power and this overcame Jem's concerns about the Ford image. The effect was a considerably cheaper car and an immediate increase in sales.

So, in 1966, the Volvo powered Marcos was discontinued. 106 had been produced in its two years. As with the earlier models, the 1800 was very popular and successful on the club circuit, the B18 engine often being bored out to two litres. Among many, many successes, it won the Freddie Dixon Memorial trophy series outright, in the hands of Chris Boulter, and several are still raced in many historic events both in this country and abroad.

To this day, the Marcos 1800 is Jem's favourite. 'In retrospect,' he says, 'I liked it better than all the later ones. It was a most relaxing car to drive and I loved the original dashboard layout; unfortunately, this proved too expensive to produce for long. By the standards of other cars around at the time, it had a really futuristic, luxurious cockpit. The first models had independent suspension all-round and there was nothing to touch it for its roadholding and the sheer controllability and flexibility it got from its great torque. Remember that most of the other fast cars around had stressed Ford engines. It had its faults, naturally; the car was noisy and the windscreen demister never worked. I was always a bit conscious, too, of that wheel falling off.'

# *CHAPTER 7*

## *FROM VOLVO TO FORD. THE BRADFORD FLOOD*

Despite Jem's sadness at seeing his old friend the Volvo 1800 go, he explains the mood of hope following in the tracks of the switch to Ford engines: 'Thank heavens the Ford image changed so rapidly because, although the 1800 Volvo engine could hardly be beaten for power and it had a lovely gearbox with overdrive, it was making the car far too expensive. The Ford 1500 GT engine's cheapness and sudden availability direct through Ford distributors, was our salvation, it really was - and what a relief! We stuck that 1500 GT lump into the car like a shot.'
But the company still felt that it should disguise the Ford name tag, so a special 'Marcos' rocker box cover was produced and the downdraught Weber carburettor was exchanged for twin Strombergs. Apart from the power unit, the only other change made was to a French polished wooden dashboard. But in the event, although this gave the car a real look of luxury, it did take hours to manufacture.

The anticipated increase in interest followed and a whole new excitement pervaded the mill as sales continued to climb. Bradford-on-Avon is a tourist centre in its own right but Marcos became an added attraction. Although the firm was flattered by all the attention it was getting, there were times when the sheer numbers of tourists became a nuisance.

The next step the company took to capitalise on this success was to launch a beefier version of the car. This, again, followed demand and resulted in the Chris Lawrence tuned 1650cc Ford-engined Marcos being unveiled at the 1967 Racing Car Show. Chris was a friend of Jem's and had been developing and racing his own tiny Deep Sanderson coupés since the early sixties. Jem asked Chris if he could get more power from the Ford block

and I think the result must have staggered even Chris, for he drove out the standard 85bhp to 120bhp, making for a very fast Marcos indeed.
It shows what a good chassis the car had in that the only modifications required to take a considerable increase in power were slightly larger front discs, slightly revised suspension and extra sound insulation to cope with the extra noise. 'The only trouble with this engine' says Jem, 'was that it was a real enthusiast's engine and I wanted something which would give customers reliability as well as performance. When on song, it went like a bird; but it did need constant tinkering. The Solex carburettor also had a habit of falling off. Nevertheless, it was successful and we made 32 of them in 1967.'
In fact, later that year, both this and the 1500 were superseded by the new Ford 1600cc crossflow engine which, in Jem's view, made the best balanced car he ever built. By that time, 82 of the 1500s had been constructed and the change in fortunes continued into 1968 when the company hit its highest production figures to then, reaching three cars per week.

●~~~●~~~●

Home business built steadily all year. The car was right for the free and cavaliering spirit of the Sixties when Andy Fairweather-Low of the pop group Amen Corner took possession of a specially modified car fitted with a stereo radio, a tape recorder (rarely found in cars in those days) and a record player(!), all topped off with a TV set fixed on runners in the passenger footwell. The colour he specified was lilac and the car soon became known at the works as the Strawberry Mousse. The Walker Brothers and the Beach Boys also bought Marcos cars.

In 1968, Standard Triumph approached the company to design a Mini based car using a fibreglass bodyshell, to be built in Hyfer. The instruction was to make the car look nothing like a Mini or, for that matter, a Marcos because all sorts of complications were being imposed on British goods imported into Israel at the time. The cars were to be built by a company called Autocars and Jem flew out to meet the managing director, Mr Schybynski, and his board. Apart from the faux pas of trying to order butter at breakfast time, his trip was a success. Despite the fact that the company was already experienced in assembling Standard Triumph vehicles and manufacturing fibreglass component car bodies, he found the works to be a shambles with apparent little concern for work or production targets. The problem cannot have been eased by the multiplicity of nationalities employed.

***One of the cars from the Israeli project which, although the operation was ill-fated, proved to be utterly reliable***

Two prototypes were made, one an estate bodied version and the other a GT, and tested to Israeli specifications. As usual with Marcos cars, they proved utterly reliable over thousands of miles of testing and were then shipped over to Hyfer accompanied by Rupert King who was to be in charge of manufacture.
Unfortunately, BMC, who had taken over Standard Triumph, chose that moment to pull the plug on the operation. This was a pity because the estate, which was taken over by Judith, Jem's then wife, drove many more thousands of miles without trouble. It was subsequently sold and still remains in this country. The GT was bought by some Americans who wanted to convert it to electric power. It went to America and has never been seen since.

Later that year, disaster struck. Jem was over in Portugal combining racing his Mini Marcos with a sales trip, when he happened to pick up a two day old copy of the *Daily Telegraph*. 'There, before my eyes,' he says, 'was a picture of the Bradford-on-Avon bridge completely under water. As this is only just downstream of the factory, I thought I had better 'phone up to see what was going on. It turned out that there had been no less than three feet of water in the assembly shop. All the parts, accessories and engines were under water but at least they had managed to get all the cars up onto

drums. By the time I called, the flooding had subsided and the panic was over. So I decided I might as well stay and enjoy a few days' holiday.' But the financial cost to the company was high; because it was so close to the river, it had not been possible to get flood insurance.
It was as a result of this flood that Don Fielding, who was with Marcos for seven years as a fibreglass moulder, claims his own particular record as the first person to have driven a Marcos in size 11 wellington boots - achieved in his haste to get one of the cars out of the way of the rising water. He describes the experience as 'hairy.' I would think that is an understatement. He also tells the story of a storeman who, first time out in the works hack 1800, found himself travelling far too fast down one of the steep hills which approach Bradford-on-Avon from every direction. Panicking, he reached for the handbrake. Unfortunately, he grabbed the pedal adjuster knob by mistake, and pulled it out of the dashboard. To finish in Don's words: 'He was also booked for speeding on the same outing - not to mention, his stay with Marcos was shortish.'

# CHAPTER 8

# THE XP MANTIS AND SPA-FRANCORCHAMPS

In February 1968, Marcos company announced that a new model was being constructed to be entered for that year's Le Mans 24 Hours. This was the Mantis, later to be renamed the XP (for Experimental Prototype) and not to be confused with the Adams's advanced design concept of the same name, of 1962. Also designed by Dennis, the XP was a tremendously exciting project and was to compete in the Group Six 3-litre GT class of the FIA Constructors' Championship.

The car was mid-engined and wedge-shaped with a general emphasis on rearward weight bias, a concept at that time just becoming fashionable. The original intention was to use a BRM engine but the company refused to co-operate and its engine was too expensive anyway, so a Repco Brabham Formula 1 power unit was chosen instead. Fuel was carried in tanks flanking the engine compartment, with the radiators set either side of the cockpit following a layout pioneered by Chaparral and Matra.

The stressed plywood monocoque construction, which had proved so successful for Marcos, was retained. Because of very deep sills, the result of using a pontoon construction, the doors had to be hinged to the windscreen. As this was very steeply raked both backwards and *in*wards to improve the aerodynamic shape, double curvature doors were needed and these were moulded in clear plastic by a local aircraft specialist. With the roof and rear bonnet sections also in clear perspex, the effect was stunning.

To create the wedge shape, the nose tapered a long way forward of the front wheels and the Adamses found an ingenious use for this: Le Mans chassis regulations required suitcase space, so, to avoid spoiling the fabulous lines, they incorporated a pull-out tray in the taper ahead of the

offside front wheel. The nose also housed an aerodynamic duct fed by a 'false' radiator.
The suspension required was of course quite different to the rigid rear axles and Triumph front suspensions at that time used in the standard cars. Fortunately, Bob Marston, a draughtsman who had previously worked with the Adamses, was now at Cooper and was able to introduce them to the parts they needed.
Dennis and Peter chose to build the XP upstairs at The Forge, the premises into which they had moved after leaving Marcos. The only problem was that, once built, they found they could not get the chassis out; there was nothing for it but to cut a hole in the floor and lower the car through.

The design was then passed to Stan Gray, at that time Marcos's development engineer, to actually build the car and it was he who breathed life into it. Spa-Francorchamps, in the Belgian Ardennes region, was chosen for the first outing of the XP with Robin Widdows and Eddie Nelson at the wheel. In the event, this proved to be too early in its development so, for once, a new Marcos car did not take the motor racing world by storm. At the last minute, Robin withdrew.

Despite the fact that he had not driven the car before, Jem decided to take over - I suspect not unwillingly. However, although Jem calls it, 'one of the most exciting experiences of my life!' it was not a comfortable one. 'The car' he explains, 'was not set up for a 6'4" driver! Due to the design, pedal space and leg-room were very restricted; in addition to that, my helmet pressed against the roof, forcing my head over at an angle. To go out and race with only a few practice laps to learn how to tame the incredible power of that Formula 1 engine stuck just behind my back added to the excitement.'

In fact the XP, having been chucked in at the deep end in a major international long distance race held in foul conditions, did remarkably well. Although three days had been allocated for practice, they only managed to get the car there the day before the race and this did not give the drivers much of a chance to get to know either car or track.

Weather conditions on race day were atrocious. The Spa circuit is tricky enough in the dry; in the wet it is deadly. That year, it was so bad that the organisers took the unprecedented step of allowing the drivers a reconnaissance lap immediately before the race. 38 cars finally started but the XP hit an immediate and most unusual problem on the first lap: there were no door seals to stop the torrential rain finding its way in and this caused a lake in the cockpit floor so bad that the car had to be brought into the pits to have a drain-hole cut in the floor! Now in last place, it climbed rapidly up to 21st position after only 10 laps.

Then Eddie spun at La Source, losing five places. The car regained two of these but by now water had got into the alternator, causing a severe misfire. To avoid damaging the engine, the team decided to call a halt - but not before a third of the field had already retired in a particularly tough race.

The press seems to have latched onto a story that the car withdrew due to oil pressure problems, the story being further embroidered by claims that the engine was losing half a litre per lap, but this is not correct. It is true that the oil pump drive had broken but this was in last minute testing at Goodwood. Luckily Stan, who was passengering Robin Widdows at the time, spotted the resulting sudden drop in oil pressure quickly enough to avert the otherwise inevitable engine blow-up, and corrected it before any damage could be done.

After its return from Spa, the expensive Repco engine was replaced with a Buick V8 and Jem took to using the car on the main roads, which must have caused some consternation among other drivers. Unfortunately, further development was put on hold by the factory flood and then there was trouble with the tax man over a claim for purchase tax on the XP. Legal or not, this was a nonsense bearing in mind that no one had actually bought the car but, as there was no way round it and the company could not afford to pay the bill, the answer was to ship the car to America. Its troubles did not end there: it was stolen, subsequently to reappear in California.

***The Marcos XP powered by a Formula 1 Repco Brabham engine***

***Testing the XP at Castle Combe***

Earlier, in March, it had been reported in the press that 'British hopes for an outright win [at Le Mans] rest on the sole Marcos BRM.' Unfortunately, 1968 was also the year of the student unrest in Paris, as a result of which the organisers, the Automobile Club de l'Ouest, decided to postpone the race from its normal June to September. By this time the XP was in America and unable to take part. Had that not happened, the XP story may have been very different.

In 1979, while surveying a property for Jem, Richard Falconer came across an unfamiliar mould lying in a roof space. 'To my great surprise', he says, 'it turned out to be the nose mould for the XP and I asked that it should be protected from Jem's penchant for throwing things away [a second chassis and body panels had already met this fate]. Pat Cuss, a friend of mine and a former mould maker for Marcos who now runs his own specialist glassfibre and light engineering business, suggested that we could build an exciting looking sportscar for hill climbing and possible production.
'We suggested to Jem that we should produce replicas of the fabled XP. He agreed with some alacrity, perhaps remembering the sensation the car had caused on its original appearance. Unfortunately, he was only able to produce a couple of photographs but kindly agreed to pay Dennis [Adams] to supervise the shape of the car as it progressed. Building cars from old photographs and people's reminiscences is not an exercise I would recommend to anyone! The only available drawings were two dreadful efforts in a 1968 copy of *Model Cars*. In fact, these had been drawn by two different draughtsmen and the variations were so enormous that *Model Cars* in desperation published them both. But this article did tell us the fact that the car was 13'1" long. Only when we had struggled for months with the construction of the car and found it quite impossible to reconcile the published dimensions with the tiny door openings, did I realise that 13'7" in Jem's handwriting could be read as 13'1"!'
Unfortunately, the bad luck which seems to have followed the XP throughout its life struck again. After months of hard work, an untimely fire put an end to this exciting project and to Richard's hopes that his redevelopment of the design would at last establish its full potential.

The original XP is still in California, sadly having never been raced again. It is completely unchanged and has not turned a wheel for more than 25 years. This car is an underrated part of Marcos history. It was an ingenious design and there is no reason to doubt that, suitably prepared and modified, it could not acquit itself well today.

# *CHAPTER 9*

## *DEBACLE AT LE MANS LEADS TO THE FIRST BIG-ENGINED PRODUCTION MARCOS*

Unable to run the XP in the 1968 Le Mans 24 Hours, Jem decided to enter a Volvo-engined Marcos for the race, to be driven by himself and John Quick, the top Jaguar 'E' Type racer of the time (and who may well have broken the record for the greatest number of wins in one season), with heart specialist Dr. Peter Taggart of the Middlesex Hospital as reserve driver.

The car was given to Stan Gray to prepare - you will remember that it was he who had done most of the development and engineering work on the original 1800 and who brought to life the XP Mantis. The standard 1800 engine was replaced by a Volvo 2-litre B20 unit and the bonnet was lengthened, giving the car an increased top speed of 155mph. To simulate as far as possible conditions at Le Mans, a suitably long straight was found on the roads of Wiltshire and this was used for testing - with strategically placed members of staff to act as lookouts, no doubt briefed to watch for police just as much as to protect passing motorists from dying of a heart attack.

Unfortunately when they got to Le Mans, the car could not reproduce its speed and failed even to qualify. 'It was far too slow along the straight' says Jem. 'I could only get 120mph out of her. We found out later that the camshaft timing was wrong; in those days, outside the factory teams, drivers did not take spare engines with them so, if your engine was not up to scratch, you were stuffed. Anyway, I was so incensed that, as soon as we got home, I locked myself away in the factory with Nick Harrison, our then sales manager, and Graham Coombes, our wood specialist, and we attacked a 1600 car and wooden chassis to make way for a 3-litre V6 Ford

Zodiac engine. Never again, I was determined, was a Marcos car going to be underpowered. A fortnight later, the job was done.'
This 'failure', much as it infuriated Jem at the time, turned out to be a blessing in disguise because it accelerated the move into the big-engined Marcos which were later to take the company into the exotic class and become its speciality.

***Jem and co-driver John Quick, the top Jaguar 'E' Type racer, beside the 1968 Le Mans 1800***

The race apart, the Le Mans car acquitted itself well that year. Despite having to stop to let an overheating differential cool off, Jem won his class and also recorded fastest lap in the Total Championship, a long distance race held on the full circuit at Snetterton.

The 750 Motor Club's Birkett Six Hour Relay Race at Silverstone also created intense excitement, being described by *Motoring News* as 'one of the most exciting races in recent years.' Teams of drivers can enter as many cars as they wish; the normal is four or six. Only rarely do they enter only two, which is just what Marcos did, the two being Jem and Barry Sewell. Despite this handicap, the team came in second but the winners, with six cars, had to break the record for the greatest number of laps covered in the six hour race in order to stay ahead of them. Jem finished up driving for four and a half of the six hours but it should be mentioned that Barry's achievement, in his one and a half hours of driving, was also considerable. They completed 307 laps and Jem broke the overall record for the greatest number of laps ever covered by one car in the race. This meant that Jem now held two endurance records in Silverstone relay races, the other from his very first race, in 1954. The length of time he has held these records are tests of endurance in themselves: the first is 40 years old and the second 24 at the time of writing!
As if the Saturday race was not enough, Jem then *drove* his car the four hours to Thruxton to take part in two races on the Sunday, one of which turned out to be a real ding-dong with Charles Blyth. Jem got past by scraping through on the *inside* at the chicane. As the inside wall is a solid metal barrier, not many drivers would have the nerve to overtake here and this moved one journalist to describe the manoeuvre as 'miraculous'. Most drivers would use a different expression!

Castle Combe is regarded as Marcos's home circuit. It was the scene that year of another exciting race, reported by *Motoring News* as 'a mini epic between two master tacticians, Jem Marsh and George Gould, and a Lotus driven by the up-and-coming Brian Colvin. They scrapped and vied for position with scant decorum, leaving the outcome in doubt to the very last lap, when the wily Marcos boss shoved everything to the floorboards to take the flag by yards from the Lotus.' The competition cannot have been tough enough because Jem followed this up with a scrap in an open category race between himself, a Lola T70 and a Ford GT40.

So although, in many ways, 1968 had been a bad year for Marcos, what with the flood, the problems with the XP and the unfortunate debacle at Le

Mans, it was an excellent one for Jem on the home circuit. Out of 17 recorded starts, he retired only twice. The resulting 15 finishes produced two outright wins, five class wins and a further five placings in the first three. On several occasions, he raced twice at the same meeting and, three times, raced on consecutive days at different circuits, usually driving the race car from one meeting to the next.

●~~~●~~~●

The Le Mans car eventually found its way to David Rattee, who started restoration of it in 1981, after it had been in storage for nine years. Despite that treatment, he reported, 'the car is absolutely sound and *the wooden chassis is as good as new - quite remarkable........*' [my italics]. Proof, if one needed it, of Frank Costin and Jem's claims of the durability of the wooden chassis.

●~~~●~~~●

The new Ford V6 car was the Marcos showpiece for the 1969 Racing Car Show and it caused tremendous excitement. The performance it offered was exceptional by any standards. With 144bhp combined with its light weight, it was more than a match for the Jaguar 'E' Type from 30mph to 100, which of course is where you want your road-going performance. In this model, the public were to see electric windows installed for the first time by a small series producer.

This car was also quite a hit with celebrities. Among many, Rod Stewart, the pop star, and John Noakes, presenter of BBC TV's programme *Blue Peter*, were customers. Another went to Beirut - did it survive the bombing? The late Sam Wanamaker had a Marcos which is reputed to have appeared in every film he made, although we have been unable to substantiate that. One film of his it did feature in was *File of the Golden Goose*, starring Yul Brynner and which was as bad as it sounds! Zoé Wanamaker, his actress daughter, was unfortunately unable to find any photographs but she did write to Jem to say how proud her father had been of his Marcos. Most unlikely of all was an order placed by a certain S. B. Knudsen of Michigan of whom you may not have heard but he was president of the Ford Motor Company at the time. This car is now believed to be in the Ford Museum.

***HRH The Duke of Edinburgh talks to Jem and the Adams brothers, at the 1969 Racing Car Show***

The year 1969 marked the end of not only a part of Marcos tradition, but a piece of automobile history. The wooden chassis *was* Marcos. Frank Costin and Jem had finally proved their case: wood did have the advantages over steel of longevity, torsional rigidity, great weight-saving and ease of repair. But two problems had cropped up. First, while once the cheap alternative, wooden chassis were now more expensive to produce than steel ones. Second, despite all the evidence to the contrary, the public would not lose its suspicion of it.

The company decided enough was enough. Jem commissioned the Adams brothers to produce a steel chassis to replace the wooden one and they came up with a light-weight design made from square-sectioned steel tube. The result was a 15 hours saving in chassis production time.

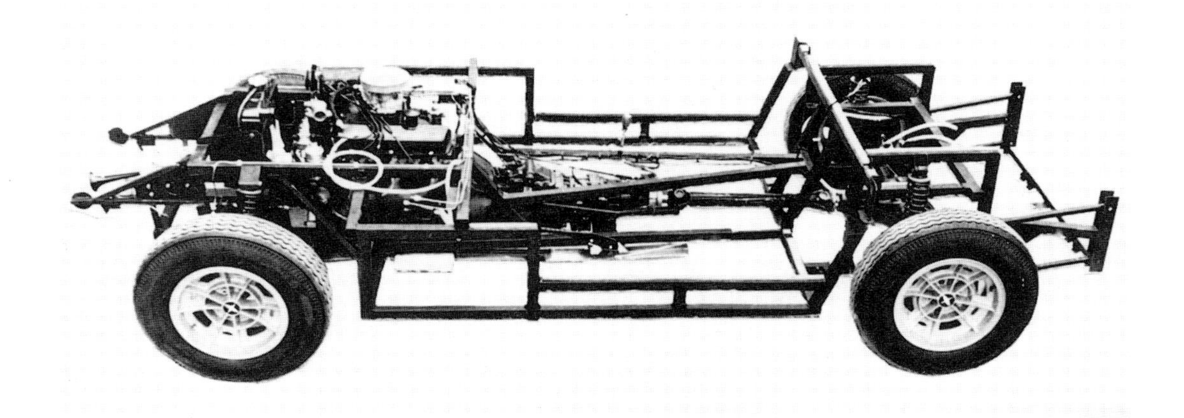

***The metal chassis introduced in 1969***

Ironically, those first steel chassis were frequently outlasted by the wooden ones they replaced, although this was a weakness subsequently cured by giving the steel chassis heavy anti-corrosion treatment. Since then, they have proved as long-lived as the rest of the car. The wooden chassis had proved to be extremely durable if properly handled.

The wooden chassis was comparatively simple to maintain. However, Rory McMath, one-time Works Manager of Marcos, still reports some horrendous examples of ignorance; for example, a well-known dealer modified one chassis with Dexion and hardboard, and another repaired a chassis undertray with ¾" shuttering ply held on by wing nuts.

Although the weight increase which resulted from converting to a steel chassis affected performance, the public were clearly happier and the boost to sales meant more employment; there were now 120 people working at Bradford-on-Avon.

•~~~•~~~•

Marcos cars were by now going all over the world. The two major export moves were launching in South Africa (through Shaun Perkins, a Durban dealer in competition parts) and in the United States of America. They could not use the Ford V6 in the USA because, as Jem says, 'It was a grotty, dirty old engine and would not pass the emission tests.' So back came Volvo into the Marcos story - this time with the straight six 164 power unit and gearbox. Although these were excellent, the engine was much heavier than the Ford V6 it replaced and this affected the car's fine balance.

In 1969, Marcos also moved to Westbury, partly so that it could cope with the American business. Here, the company made about 250 Volvo-engined cars, together with 11 powered by the Triumph 2.5-litre unit which, although they proved to be very nice, smooth and economical, were not fast by Marcos standards. Ford Corsair GT V4 engines were also used, but these turned out to be incompatible with the car. Designed in its original form for the Transit van, this engine was too low revving for the final drive ratio of the Marcos and the result was that drivers compensated by over-revving the engine, with inevitably disastrous results.

Until 1968, the company had given no model names to anything except the Mini Marcos. Although models acquired their own nicknames, they were never officially baptised anything except 'Marcos'. The departure from this tradition was the XP Mantis. That project having ended, the company decided to use the Mantis name again when it launched a new model for the 1969 Earls Court Motor Show.
You might think that this was because the new model had its origins in the old but it did not; it looked, and was, nothing like the 1968 racer. For a start, the engine was in front of the driver, not behind him. Secondly, this was a road-going 2+2 car. The only similarity was that a wedge-shaped design was chosen, but that is as far as it went.

***The Marcos Mantis, introduced in 1969***

Nevertheless, as with all Dennis's designs, it was well ahead of its time. In prototype form, it was fitted with a Ford V6 unit but, for production, the Triumph 2.5-litre fuel injection engine was preferred.
'Colin Chapman's face was a picture when he saw it, 'Jem recalls. 'He had already started work on what was to become the Lotus Eclat but it was years away from fruition and here we were with a car along exactly the same lines!' Dennis, in fact, had taken only nine months to develop it from start to manufacture. In the end, although the press did not treat the car kindly, 32 were made during the course of 1971 and sold easily to Marcos enthusiasts.

●~~~●~~~●

Then, in 1971, everything seemed to pile in and conspire against Jem. The cost of developing the Mantis is often blamed for the company's financial problems at this time but this is not so: every model made was sold. There are times in many endeavours when fate seems to take a hand and, no matter what you do, your every action seems determined not to succeed. There is not much one can do in these situations except to fight on and hope that one can win through.

The first problem to occur was that the move to a new purpose-built factory in Westbury interrupted operations far more than expected; in fact production stopped entirely for several weeks. The second blow fell when the first 27 cars shipped to America were impounded by US customs. Companies which made fewer than 500 vehicles a year were exempt from the strict US emission controls but customs could not believe that a company with a production under that figure was capable of shipping 27 cars in one go for export. It could, but only by tying up a great deal of capital. So the US operation collapsed, leaving Marcos £30,000 worse off on the deal. This despite the enthusiasm of the American motoring press; for example, *Car And Driver* headlined with, 'Mothers, hide your daughters! Marcos has arrived' and went on to say that the Marcos was 'perfect for a customer who demands exclusivity. Jags and Corvettes, which cost about the same, are fine, but everybody, including off-duty cops[!], drives them.'

The third, and worst, problem was that the UK self-assembly car market collapsed when the new Value Added Tax replaced the old purchase tax. Although component car companies (unlike manufacturers of completed cars) had been exempt from both purchase and car tax, VAT was applied to all cars. This was followed by new, worldwide safety and emission regulations which were horrendously expensive for low volume constructors to meet. Finally, 1970 was the year of the oil crisis and this had severe a knock on effect on the whole car market in 1971.

Extreme cash flow problems resulted and Jem decided that the answer was to sell out to Hebron & Medlock Bath Engineering Limited. After only six months trading, the company called in the receiver, using its debenture to sell off enough of the assets to cover the initial investment. The Rob Walker Group purchased the remaining assets, only to hold a big sale at the factory to sell off as much of the stock and as many of the body units as it could. Under new management, Rob Walker then set up the new Marcos company in a Romney unit on the present Westbury site.

***The sign of decline as Jem feeds birds nesting in a dormant Marcos!***

***Jem in a 1300 Fastback at Thruxton*** (Courtesy John Gaisford)

•~~~•~~~•

Despite all this trauma, Jem kept up a busy season on the circuits. He had found the ex-Jackie Stewart Ugly Duckling lying unused under a tarpaulin outside Chris Lawrence's garage in Astwood Mews, London. It was, he says, 'just a box of bits' and he bought it for £250. But, no matter how good a driver is, he cannot win without fast, reliable machinery. David Pickford now came into the story to take over the rebuilding and preparation of the car. He was doing an apprenticeship with Jem and worked nearly every evening to keep the car in winning trim, becoming in the process, under Jem's guidance, a superb race mechanic. Jem says that David played a vital part in helping him to win both the Classic Car and the Historic Sportscar championships.

# *CHAPTER 10*

## *THE MINI MARCOS, LE MANS AND 'FLIRT'*

The Mini Marcos story began in 1965. Still part of the company's production today, it is the complete opposite in philosophy of the big-engined 3.9-litre Mantaras and 5-litre LM500s which spearhead the current Marcos effort.
In fact, since the company was launched, it has steadily moved to bigger and bigger cars and engines. The Mini Marcos is the exception; designed to take Mini components, it is a throwback in engine size to the Gullwings with which it started. To date, this is the only Marcos, since the very first Costin model, not to have been designed by Dennis Adams. Many people call it ugly although, like the first Gullwings, there is something compellingly attractive about its ugliness. Among other achievements, Marcos could claim, if it wished, to make both the most and the least attractive models in the car market.

●~~~●~~~●

The Mini Marcos nearly did not come the company's way at all. The idea was borne out of a meeting with Dizzy Addicott, a test pilot-cum-racing driver, at the 1963 Racing Car Show. Dizzy had built a Mini special called a D.A.R.T. (Dizzy Addicott Racing Team), by cutting the top off a Mini van and sticking his own design of body onto it. Dizzy commissioned Falcon Shells, that other specialist car builder in whom Greville Cavendish had a financial interest, to build the shell.

Jem, however, did not agree with the brief Falcon had been given. Believing that the car was clearly best suited to the price sensitive end of the market, he felt that the method of construction would make it too expensive. He also felt that the design should be taken one stage further by building the complete body out of fibreglass. So he asked Malcolm Newell to collaborate on a new design.

***The original drawing of the Mini Marcos***

Malcolm was a brilliant designer with a character as colourful as Jem's own; when he died in 1994, he was, at his request, buried in his own garden! Apart from the Mini Marcos, he also did work on AC Cobra bodies, but his real claim to fame was the unique and remarkable Quasar, a high performance motorcycle with body, about as close to a two-wheeled car as it is possible to get. The Quasar was definitely one British solution to the foreign motorcycles which we allowed to decimate our industry - in fact, his follow-up, the Phasar, holds the British record for road-going machines at 161mph. Although hundreds of machines were ordered from all over the world, the stupidity of British banks, business and government showed yet

another inability to recognise and support a great British product and it failed.
As reported in *Motorcycle Sport*, his great friend Royce Creasey said of Malcolm that many bureaucrats regarded him 'as a dangerous maniac.........It would do the country no harm whatsoever if such people [i.e., bureaucrats] were routinely terrorised by the likes of Malcolm Newell. His lack of deference and respect was not only healthy, it should be mandatory.' It should add greatly to the appeal of the incredibly successful Mini Marcos to know that it was constructed by such a man.

To keep costs to an absolute minimum for the customer, Jem told Malcolm to produce a monocoque body/chassis which would accept all Mini parts 'straight', that is to say, without further modification. This was a wise move; because the Mini Marcos was so affordable and easy to build, it was destined to become easily the most successful of all the Mini based component cars in terms of sales, longevity and racing results. Many people think the Mini Marcos is so ugly because it is badly designed but that is not so - it had to be to retain the original radiator, a deliberate move to keep the cost down.
Typical of Jem, once the decision was made, the new model was launched in double quick time - in fact, well before the Dizzy Addicott car - and at the incredible price of only £199 for the body unit and windscreen. It was an immediate success; the first advertisement in *Motor Sport* alone brought in 144 enquiries. Its official launch was at the 1966 Racing Car Show, although several cars had already been sold by the end of 1965.

The car had its first race at Castle Combe. As was now becoming normal practice with a new Marcos model, the car annihilated the competition in its maiden run. Driven by Geoff Mabbs, it was built and race prepared by Janos 'Jan' Odor of Janspeed Engineering in Salisbury, and completed only at midnight the night before the meeting. Geoff therefore had no time to drive the car before the practice session for the race. Even so, he was fastest in practice and, in the race, went straight into the lead. After only 10 laps, he had lapped every other car except one and, in heavy rain, came in almost one minute and 22 seconds ahead of the second placed car.

Powered by a 1275cc Cooper 'S' engine, and race prepared by BMC's special tuning department in Abingdon (which had no idea for what the car was being prepared), a French owned Mini Marcos was entered for the 1966 Le Mans race. This was to be driven by Jean-Louis Marnat and Claude Ballot-Lena who later became very well-known as a racer of Porsches. Jem went to have a look and, as usual when he gets involved, the event ended up by being quixotic but successful:
'I had a quick snoop round the car and found that it was lashed together with wire. So I got hold of the owners and worked with them to get it right. Alec Issigonis [the designer of the Mini and also, incidentally, of the Morris Minor] got to see the car and hated it on sight. He wanted nothing to do with it, but he soon had his nose put out of joint. Although I spent most of the race going round apologising for the car because it showed me up too, the damn thing went on and on and eventually finished - the only British car that year to do so!'
An unattributed press report sums up the feeling of pride well: 'Anyone who watched the Le Mans 24 hour race last year on the television will surely remember the commentator saying on the Sunday that a small kit-built British car had become the darling of the crowds. Right near the end one caught a flashing glimpse of the travel-stained little machine, running like a train towards the end of one of the hardest races in the world. This, of course, was the Mini Marcos.'
Once again, Jem experienced the heady feeling of success as telegrams of congratulation poured in. His favourite, from 'Barbra, Roger and Tim' reads:

'Congratulations Marcos Mighty,
Keep your hands off the Contessa's nighty.'

The car completed 2152 miles at an average speed of almost 90mph in the 24 hours. Once the engine freed up properly, it went even faster, lapping consistently at 100mph. But perhaps what pleased Jem more was that the Mini Marcos was by far the cheapest car in the race. Again, he had proved his incredible ability to create fast, reliable, competitive machinery virtually hot off the press and untested. Unfortunately, this car The Le Mans car came to an undeserved end. It was stolen from its owner and has never been seen since. If it were ever found, the value to Marcos enthusiasts of this plucky little car would be high so Jem expects that a rash of false claimants will eventually hit the market.

***The Marnat/Ballot-Lena Mini Marcos which did so well at Le Mans in 1966***
(Courtesy Geoffrey Goddard)

In 1967, Jem introduced the Mini Marcos to South Africa, through a father and son team, the Raubenheimers, who set up a factory to make units in Natal, under the name Marcos Cars (South Africa). While there, he and Brian Raubenheimer took the opportunity to race a 1.3-litre Mini Marcos in the Kyalami Nine Hours, one of the world's great long distance events. They finished 15th, which does not sound much until you see who and what beat them: Jacky Ickx and Brian Redman in a 5.7-litre Mirage-Ford... a 5.9-litre Lola-Chevrolet... a 4.7-litre Ford GT40 co-driven by Mike Hailwood... a 2-litre Porsche Carrera... David Piper and Richard Attwood in a 4.4-litre Ferrari ... two 3.3-litre Ferraris... a 1.5-litre Alpine-Renault... a 1.8-litre Porsche RSK... a 1.6-litre Lotus Elan... and a 1.6-litre Alfa Romeo Giuila Sprint GT among them. Among the cars they beat were, amusingly, two 1800 Volvos... three 4.7-litre Ford-engined cars... two 5.5-litre Lola-Chevrolets (one driven by Frank Gardner and Mike Spence)... a 3.3-litre Ferrari... 2-litre Triumph TR6, Porsche and Elfin... 1.6-litre GSM Dart and two Alfa Romeos. Not a bad collection of scalps for a tiny 1.3-litre car!

***Jem at the Kyalami Nine Hour Race, 1967***

***Jacquie Bond-Smith, Jackie Smith and Joey Cooke, the FLIRT Team drivers***

The 1967 season also saw the debut of the First Ladies' International Racing Team (FLIRT), consisting of Jacquie Bond-Smith, Jackie Smith (no relation) and Joey Cooke, and driving a Mini Marcos in the 1000kms race at the Nürburgring in Germany. Unfortunately, a conrod bolt failed and put them out of the race. But the Mini Marcos still had a successful meeting, with Michael Garton and Paddy McNally winning the 1300cc prototype class in the car which, later that year, was to enter Le Mans, and Guy Edwards and Peter Anslow coming second in class in their 1293cc car.

***The FLIRT Mini Marcos at the Nürburgring, 1967*** (Courtesy H.P. Seufert)

Mugello, in Italy, was the venue for the FLIRT's second race. There was no class for the Marcos 1300 cars so they were put into the 2-litre prototype category which was dominated by Porsche Carreras. The FLIRT came in a very creditable fifth behind the Porsches; one place ahead of the men's team consisting of Mike Garton and Tim Lalonde - but they had lost their petrol filler cap and the resultant spillage of fuel meant a refuelling stop on every lap. At one stage, they were forced to refuel at a garage in one of the villages on the circuit! Next outing was at Enna in Sicily where the men's 1300 was again put into the 2-litre prototype class. They were beaten only by a 2-litre Porsche, but beat a gaggle of Alfa Romeo TZs.

Jem also entered and drove a Mini Marcos in the 1967 Le Mans race, partnered by Chris Lawrence. This incredible little car topped 141mph down the Mulsanne Straight in practice and qualified. Even at that speed, Jem recalls that the airstream of the Ford GT40s overtaking would physically 'bump' the Mini Marcos sideways. At seven o'clock in the morning, Jem and Chris had the car certified as passed by the scrutineers.

'Then' says Jem, 'Chris and I went off for our medicals. When we returned, there was this Frenchman, complete with beret, rubbing the scrutineers' label off! After much expostulation, we were informed that the windscreen was two centimetres out on rake and height. While I was arguing in broken French that this was exactly the same as the model which had passed scrutineering the previous year and what was two centimetres anyway, Chris noticed something: the first reserve car, which would gain a place in the race if any cars were eliminated, was a Hrubon entered by the Frenchman who had run the Mini Marcos the previous year with such success. Then the penny dropped and we realised there was no point in arguing. We had until seven o'clock the next morning to correct the problem. It seemed impossible, but Chris and I got the car back to the chateau where we were staying as fast as we could. There, the chateau owner showed us to his workshop: a rudimentary affair with just one light. In front of the workshop was a dead pig with its throat cut, dumped into a wheelbarrow full of offal.'

When the Marcos team had first arrived at the chateau, it was very happy at being shown into bedrooms which had been beautifully laid out with Louis XVI furniture. But the joy was short-lived: two days later a block-booking of BP people arrived and the team was relegated to an annexe with school-type mattresses on damp beds and yet more of the dead pigs outside. In fact, it did not matter too much because Jem and David James, the managing director of one of the late Maxwell Joseph's hotel groups, had to work all day and all night to change the height and rake of the windscreen, assisted by Mike Treutlein.

***The Mini Marcos at Le Mans, 1967, before the windscreen was moved forward...........***
(Courtesy Photo Beroul-Le Mans)

***...........and how it looked afterwards***

'At seven o'clock, much to the amazement of the French scrutineers, we got the car back. A French newspaper christened this event, "The return of the wounded bird." With the windscreen angled more upright, the car looked even more awful than it had been designed but at least, try as they might, and they spent ages at it, the scrutineers could find no fault with it.'
A two centimetre modification does not sound much but it was enough to cut the car's top speed from 141 to 138mph. Nevertheless, the car was well up in the race until, after four hours, the transfer gears failed. A sad end to a tremendous effort.

Greater success came in the Enna Cup that year, when Jem came second in class. Held in central Sicily, around Lake Pergusa, this race was reputed to be the toughest in the world. 'It was searing hot that day,' Jem reflects. 'I managed only three laps in practice before the engine overheated. A bolt had fallen out of the cylinder head allowing all the water to escape. The organisers were fantastic - they stopped practice and had all the course cars driving round the circuit looking for the bolt! In the meantime, I was just starting to get visions of having to scour Palermo to get a new one machined when I managed to unearth a spare one in the VW transporter.
'We had a great race and I managed to beat quite a few Ferraris. The collection of the prize money was a story in itself; I had to climb up these steps in the back streets of Palermo, at the top of which were these menacing looking people who piled money into my hands. I have no idea what it was for but I took it anyway.'
'On the way home, we all, my wife and two sons and I, had only the transporter to sleep in. One night, we got chased off our camp site by wild dogs. Then I got laid down by sunstroke. As Barbara could not drive the transporter, the Marsh family came to a halt while I spent a few days under the transporter recovering. All in all, a very exciting trip!'
I don't think anyone except Jem would find sunstroke exciting.

•~~~•~~~•

In 1968, the Mini Marcos followed in the footsteps of big brother when Corgi Toys launched it as a model. Innovation by Marcos also went into innovation by Corgi. As their advertising literature proclaimed:

'For the first time ever in die-cast model cars! "Take-off" wheels and four built-in "Golden Jacks"! Long ago Corgi engineers realised that Corgi collectors and enthusiasts would dearly love to be able to change the wheels on their model cars. Tyres have been removable and replaceable since the earliest days of die-cast models. But, only now has a solution been found to the technical difficulties involved in providing removable wheels.'

With four built-in operating jacks and interchangeable wheels, the advertising literature goes on to tell us that this represents:

'a revolution in scale model car design.'

When Jem bought back the Marcos assets from the Rob Walker Group in 1976, he sold on the Mini Marcos designs and moulds to Harold Dermott of D&H Fibreglass Techniques of Lancashire. Harold went on to make another 335 Mini Marcos before, in 1981, replacing it with his own car, the Midas. D&H ceased trading in December 1989. In this event, Jem's agreement with Harold was that the Mini Marcos name and moulds would revert to being the property of Marcos. And so, in May 1991, after a 10 year absence from production, the model was relaunched at the National Kit Car Show at Stoneleigh, during which members of the Mini Marcos Owners' Club succeeded in building a complete car in only 24 hours.

***Members of the Mini Marcos Owners' Club nearing the end of their 24 hour build***

The 1990s saw the Mini-mad Japanese taking a keen interest in this car and it was exhibited at the Tokyo Motor Show. For them, the company built complete cars with air conditioning, engines designed to run on lead free fuel and catalytic converters.

●~~~●~~~●

Perhaps the greatest success of the Mini Marcos was seen in 1978, 12 years after it was first launched. A fiery 1460cc engined car not only won the BARC's Modsport championship outright but also broke several of Sir Henry Seagrave's long-standing British speed records as well: the Flying Start 500 metres, one kilometre, quarter mile and one mile records, all at an average of around 150mph. These records are still unbroken at the time of writing.

Apart from this, the Mini Marcos has been, and still is, a phenomenally successful competition car, moving Laurie Caddell to describe Neil Roscoe's car, in *Sports Car Monthly* as: 'one of the most successful sports racing cars of all time.' That was written in 1986, about just one of the many Mini Marcos which were winning races well before then and are still doing so today.

***The 1991 Tokyo Motor Show***

The whole character of the car lends itself to doing exciting things. Roger Garland, the secretary of the Mini Marcos Owners Club instances just one of these: in 1990, he successfully completed a trip into the Arctic Circle and back, a journey of over 4,000 miles over sometimes harsh terrain, with hardly a problem.

The Mini Marcos now in its Mark V version, is still competitive in race meetings, 28 years after it was launched. Although now sporting a front spoiler and wider track, it looks still very much the same. But, over the years, it has established a great reputation in its own right. Produced with cheapness in mind, it certainly qualified as 'heap of the week' on second hand forecourts for years. But quality will out and, today, good examples retain their secondhand values remarkably well.

So the Marcos reputation for longevity, endurance and competition success is based not just on the cars for which the company is best known now - the big engined sports GT models - but on two models at completely opposite ends of the road going spectrum.

## *CHAPTER 11*

## *THE PHOENIX RISES AGAIN: THE '50s DREAM STORMS INTO THE '90s*

In 1972, at the age of 42 and with just £200 to his name, Jem rented the Romney unit next door to Rob Walker's premises, to set up a spares and restoration service for Marcos owners. This unit was to be the first of the several Romney units from which the company still operates.
Business soon flourished to the point where he was able to buy a car sales business in Warminster, Wiltshire, and take on a Datsun dealership. But, after three and a half years, he had had enough of the importer's dictatorial attitude and terminated the franchise. Datsun dealerships were then much prized, so this was almost unheard of, but Jem is beholden to no one. He replaced this with a Lancia dealership and the move paid off - he was soon able to open a second one in Bath.

Jem re-acquired the Marcos name and moulds from the Rob Walker Group in 1976, but without having the capital needed to restart manufacture. He was soon joined by Rory MacMath. Rory was to stay with Jem for the next 16 years, until 1992, eventually becoming Works and Stores Manager.

During this period, Marcos might have been history to any outsider, it was not to Jem; he was determined to come back and, in 1981, his success in these activities meant that he was at last able to start making Marcos cars again. Considering it was 10 years since the car had last been produced, it says something for the enduring quality of Dennis's design that it could be relaunched virtually as it had left off. Club Marcos International and the Marcos Owners' Club also played their part in keeping the marque's spirit alive and healthy in the intervening years. It is to their credit that the name was still so well known that only one press release was enough to get orders going and the company found that it had immediately tapped into a latent demand for the Marcos, still there a decade on.

***A concept car drawn by Dennis in 1981***

For three years, the company stuck with the Ford 1600 and 3-litre V6 engines but then, in 1984, came the move which was to take it into the exotic car class - the launch of a Marcos with a 3.5-litre Rover V8 engine. The timing could not have been more appropriate because 1984 was also the 25th anniversary of the company. Capable of 0 to 60mph in 5.7 seconds, 0 to 100 in 16 seconds and with a top speed of 150mph, it was faster than all but the most expensive Italian cars.

This introduction to the sportscar superleague also needed a suitably colourful name and one was found: Mantula, created by a corruption of Mantis and Tarantula. Its launch created such an impact that Norman

Tebbit, in his opening speech at the 1985 Motorfair at Earls Court, listed Marcos alongside Rolls-Royce and Jaguar as examples of the best in the British car industry.

The Marcos shape needed no change for its new image; both style and quality of finish were already there. But what about the need to accommodate the very large increase in power from 120 to 190bhp? Surely, Dennis would need to heavily modify the design to cope? In fact, not. Just as with the considerable step up in output from the 1500cc to the 1650 Lawrence-tuned Ford engine, he had to make very few changes.
All the car needed was a larger air intake at the front to cope with some cooling problems (which, as a side-benefit, created the shark-like, bared teeth nose), a widening of the rear track by four inches to take a stronger axle, and a front spoiler to counteract the lift which was now occurring at high speeds.

But the most incredible result of incorporating the new power unit was to create an almost exact 50-50 weight distribution between front and back. If anyone criticises Marcos for not following the mid-engined route of the German and Italian supercars, the answer is that the company did not have to. The purpose of mid- or some rear-engined cars is to achieve near balanced weight distribution between front and back and Dennis did this with a front-engined layout.

The new car achieved everything the company wanted, and more. Even though it matches its Italian and German competitors on performance, the Marcos is generally much easier to drive. It has excellent all-round vision, the only problem being that the long nose tapers out of view and creates difficulties in parking, but no lover of exotics would mark it down for that. To the continuing surprise of most motoring journalists, who expect performance cars to be intractable in traffic, the Marcos is truly a gentle 'giant'; in fact, although the ego of some Marcos owners might have you believe otherwise, it does not require a hairy chested he-man to control it.

*The 3.5-litre Mantula, the first Rover-engined Marcos*

Early Mantulas had only three problems. First, they had a harsh, choppy ride but, of course, all performance cars of the time suffered from that. This was corrected in 1989 by replacing the live rear axle with the present independent suspension. Second, the boot was tiny. Again, this was, and is, normal in a performance GT. However, the change to independent rear suspension also cured that. Lyn is a keen golfer so, when she came along, the boot space assumed more importance to Jem and. by the time the Mantula was replaced by the Mantara, the boot would comfortably take *two* full sets of golf clubs and two trolleys - virtually unheard of in GT circles! Many open cars have boot space only until you take the hood down; this then fills the boot. The Spyder hood designed to fold flat so that, even when down, it takes up no boot space. The LM500 will take even more luggage and competes with many a saloon for stowage capacity.

Interior misting up is another problem which plagues many sportscars. The Mantula was launched with a heated rear window as standard. In 1986, Marcos became the first small series car manufacturer to fit a heated *front* windscreen as well and included this as standard equipment. The company followed this by offering air conditioning as a complete solution to misting.

Sportscars can suffer equally from overheated footwells which may be fine in winter but are most unpleasant on those warm days when many sportscar drivers most want to use their cars. The ingenious solution on the Marcos was to fit fans at the bottom of the footwells and this, coupled with air conditioning, makes the atmosphere of the car as comfortable as any luxury saloon, even in extremes of temperature.
The last model of the Mantula, when it was replaced by the Mantara in 1994, looked very similar to the first one of 1984, but this hid the fact that there had been intensive detail development of parts during the intervening years - so much so that almost every part of the original model had been superseded. The standard 3.5-litre twin carburettored Rover engine was later uprated with the introduction of the fuel-injected 3.5-litre Vitesse unit, and again by the 3.9-litre version when that became available. Power went up in that period from 190bhp to 300 in the 'Sport' version, necessitating continual improvements to the suspension, braking and steering systems.

But the original design was so good that these were detail rather than fundamental changes.

The car is now so well set up that attempts to improve road holding with wider wheels actually decrease performance! As Jem says with great frustration: 'I *keep* telling customers not to monkey around with wheel sizes but they just go ahead and do it anyway!' In fact, the works refuses to fit anything other than the recommended tyre widths to road-going cars.

All the Marcos models have proved themselves to be exceptionally reliable, a tribute to the craftsmanship which goes into them. My own current one, a 1985 Mantula coupé, has done 130,000 virtually trouble-free miles in three years, almost entirely on business, but I am only one of many high mileage Marcos drivers; back in 1983, *Thoroughbred & Classic Cars*, while profiling two drivers who had travelled more than 125,000 miles, recorded: 'Interestingly, many owners use these precious cars every day, rejecting mothballs.' The highest mileage car we have been able to trace is one approaching 300,000 miles!

●~~~●~~~●

Marcos may have been taking a 'breather' from manufacture, but this did not show on the track where Marcos cars were still winning. In 1976, Jonathan Palmer, after a brief flirtation with a frog-eye Sprite, bought a 3-litre Marcos Ford V6 to compete in the BARC Modsports Championship. Despite a late start due to an unreliable engine, he finished up with five wins and second place overall to John Cooper. His following season proved even more successful. Overcoming another late start, the trainee doctor had an amazing 15 class wins from 20 starts and broke five lap records. Winning his class easily, he also came second overall - and that only because the winner had had the advantage of a full season. (He went on to race in Formula 1 and sportscars at World Championship level).

In 1978, Jem, driving the ex-Jackie Stewart Ugly Duckling, won the Classic Sportscar Championship outright. In 1979, despite literally breaking the car in two in a crash at Brands Hatch, he finished second in the Classic Car Championship.

In the 1980 season, he was back to his winning ways, taking the Thoroughbred Championship outright. This was a competition run by the Aston Martin Owners' Club and it was a shock for these exotic cars to be beaten in their own championship by the little Wooden Wonder!

In the following year, Roger Ealand won the Classic Sportscar Championship outright in an 1800, beating the likes of AC Cobras and Lotus 23s.
Mark Hales, in a 1969 wooden chassised 3-litre, gained 14 pole positions, 10 outright wins and four lap records in 24 starts. On top of this, he recorded the first 100mph lap of Castle Combe in a modsports car. In fact, the only thing which came between him and the championship was a mid-season shunt. This car was rebuilt in the early eighties with a supercharged Volvo B20 engine and is now racing in the Swedish Modsport series.

Marcos 1800s continued their successes with two further outright championship successes in 1984: Roger Ealand again won the Classic Sportscar Championship and Jem took the Bellini Historic Sportscar Championship. In addition, the new Mantula kept up the Marcos tradition of new models winning first time out, this time in the hands of Richard Gamble, and despite the selection of first, third and fifth gears being something of a lottery. This success continued into 1985, with class wins for both Roger and Jem in the same two championships but Jem also taking third in class in the Classic Sportscar Championship.

***Racing Marcos through the ages line up at Donnington Park, 1985***

***Jem leads the field on the way to winning the Classic Sportscar Championship in 1978*** (Courtesy John Gaisford)

***Jem winning the Pontins Trophy outright in 1980, beating 3.8 Jaguars and 'E' Types***
(Courtesy John Gaisford)

***Richard Gamble's Modsports Marcos, ex-Jonathan Palmer car***

●~~~●~~~●

In 1986, the company launched the Spyder, the open topped version of the Mantula coupé. Open cars often look great with the hood down but the effect can be completely ruined with it up. The appearance of some, like the pleasing Morgan and the Caterham, are so completely spoilt when the hood

is in use that any self-respecting owner simply refuses to use it. Being drenched in rain is, to them, more acceptable than driving in what appears to be a car with a tent on top of it.
This criticism cannot be levelled at the Spyder which is arguably the most attractive open car around with the hood down and, with it up, rivals in looks the coupé version. On top of that, and again unlike many soft tops, the conversion is very effective, being described by one motoring journalist as, 'the best that we have ever encountered with the possible exception of the Mercedes SL sports.' With the hood down, there is little buffeting even at high speeds and, when up, it actually works as it should. Indeed, one sometimes forgets that this is a soft top, an illusion strengthened by the interior padding and lining of the hood. Ease of erection is important for soft tops and here, again, the Spyder scores well; unlike many others, it can be erected and put down in less than one minute.

The creation of the open body was relatively easy. The body being unstressed anyway, all that was needed was substantial stiffening of the windscreen and chassis. The real problem could have been the styling but, once again, Dennis Adams worked his usual magic and the Spyder looks more as if it was styled from scratch as an open car in its own right than being based on the coupé with the top chopped off.

•~~~•~~~•

Through the 1980s, the company had prospered but it was not easy; specialist or small series car producers are susceptible to sudden shifts in economic conditions and the dividing line between success and failure is always narrow - it is inherent in the business. If asked to name one quality car company which was recession proof, most people would have chosen either Rolls Royce or Porsche, yet just look at how badly both faired when the recession bit. Traditionally, small series producers tend to be 'one product' companies and this puts them even more at the mercy of a downturn in the economy, or a change in consumer taste. In the late '80s, Marcos was in just this vulnerable position, having only the top of the market Mantula to rely on. As the recession deepened, Jem realised that it was not good business sense to simply rely on that.

In addition, the company had not yet obtained type approval and this meant that its market was always self-limiting. However, it was not generating the profit necessary to cover the high costs involved. Apart from anything else, obtaining type approval requires crash testing as well as a nightmare of expensive, time consuming bureaucracy, something with which the impatient Jem is not good at dealing.

In addition, ever more sophisticated competition meant ever more expensive research and development were required. This, coupled with the cost of seeking type approval, resulted in Jem, for the first time in his life, setting out on the venture capital trail. It was to take four years to find the investment he wanted mainly because, like all of us who seek to raise business capital, he had his time wasted by those pseudo financiers who make a full-time career of pretending that they are in the investment business when they are not. Some of these are conmen who hope that, by promising money to you, they can get money out of you to 'sweeten the deal' or to 'oil the wheels'. Others have money but have no intention of placing it; they get a sick pleasure out of stringing serious and sometimes desperate businesspeople along. The trouble is, pursuing each avenue can take a long time, sometimes months, and, even if you are suspicious of a potential investor's motives, you cannot afford not to see each one through in case you are wrong. In hindsight, they make good stories, but they are anything but pleasant at the time.

The first of these people was a Mr 'U'. He came onto the Marcos stand at the Birmingham Motor Show in 1988, having apparently been piloted in from his home in Switzerland, in his own private aircraft. He told Jem that, when he was younger, he had had to struggle with under-capitalisation. He now wanted to help a company in the same position and had substantial funds available. During discussions, he happened to mention that he had an Aston Martin so, when he left the stand, Jem went to make enquiries of that company's sales manager, who confirmed that Mr 'U' had indeed bought several Aston Martins. Reassured by this, Jem arranged for a further meeting with Mr 'U', at the Marcos works. Here, he bought a Marcos on the spot. He also told Jem that he would later need £12,000 from Jem in order to release the large amounts of money being considered, from the Swiss banks.

Some time later, after a lot of phone calls from Mr 'U', often at peculiar times and from which nothing seemed to materialise, Jem started to get worried. Mr 'U' had claimed to be married to an Adidas heiress and had told Jem where he lived, in a large house outside Geneva. As it happened, Jem's sister was also living near Geneva so he asked her to go along and check up. She found a large house all right but large guard dogs prevented her from getting in.

Then Mr 'U' phoned Jem to say that the releasing deal was now in place and he was flying someone over to collect the £12,000. This was followed up by a visit to Geneva by Jem to sign his contract with Mr 'U'.

Jem then got a phone call from a couple in Zürich. Mr 'U' had inveigled £40,000 out of them, ostensibly to fund up a big oil deal with Nigeria. Having collected the money, he had left his Marcos in their care and flown off to Lagos. The couple then became suspicious. Unfortunately for him, a search of the car revealed the log book still in the glove box, and still in Jem's name.

The result of that was a phone call to Jem and Lyn who caught the next plane to Zürich where they met the couple for dinner. While actually in the restaurant, the couple had another phone call from Mr 'U', going through exactly the same empty promises routine with which Jem had become familiar. While no one could prove anything, Jem and Lyn decided to play safe and bring back Mr 'U's' Marcos with them - its resale value would cover their £12,000 'investment' in him.

'That trip back,' Jem recalls, 'was an eerie one. Bearing in mind we were not sure that we were in the right, we had this nasty feeling of being followed! Had we been stopped, there would have been some embarrassed explaining to do!' So nervous were they that, at a lunch stop in the middle of nowhere, Jem locked the car keys in the boot. He forced it open with a screwdriver so, for the rest of the journey, they had to put up with the boot-lid flapping up and down.

In the event, Mr 'U' did prove to be dishonest. Although Jem recouped his losses, the Zürich couple were not so lucky: they were almost bankrupted.

Mr 'S' was the next so-called financier to appear, in 1989. Jem carries on the story. 'He came from Canada. His trip did not start very well; he'd bought a Lagonda in Switzerland, fully intending to sell it at a big profit in the UK. Unfortunately for him, his timing was bad - it was at the time of the crash in the classic car market and he got only half what he'd paid for it! Anyway, he told us that he wanted to buy the whole factory - not only that, but he was looking at buying Castle Combe [the race circuit] as well. The upshot was that contracts were signed and he paid us £18,000 deposit with the rest to follow when he got back to Canada. I'd just completed a very special 1800 for myself for the Classic Sportscar Championship. Although it wasn't for sale, he was so insistent about it that in the end I sold that to him as well. Actually, he did very well with it, winning several races and beating much heavier machinery like Mustangs and the big American sportscars.'

Mr 'S' had returned to Canada with the promise that he would handle the North American and Canadian market, including getting Marcos through the various national regulations. As he had already spent a fair bit of money with Jem, and was competing so conspicuously with the car, it was more with a sense of frustration than doubt that the company waited for the balance of the money so that it could start the process of getting type approval in the UK.

Then Jem found out that, when Mr 'S' had been over in the UK, he had also approached Lotus and convinced the management that he ought to be its Canadian importer. To tie up with a competitor is strange behaviour for anyone wanting to buy a company, so Jem did more research, only to discover that Mr 'S' had been involved with the Canadian importer of Lamborghinis. 'I think I should warn you,' the Canadian importer told Jem over the phone, 'that everyone here is after him. If anyone does catch up with him, he is liable to get knee-capped!'

Fortunately, the contract had been carefully drawn up so that the £18,000 which Mr 'S' had already paid was treated as a non-returnable deposit and, because he had never completed his side of it, no shares were ever issued. Later, Jem was to get a letter from Mr 'S' to say that he was now president of a raceway on Vancouver Island, called Mountain Aire. As Jem put it, 'These people never give up!' On this particular occasion, Jem came out on top.

Mr 'B's' approach was different; he is one of those so-called businesspeople who takes the deal through to the last stage and then, just when he thinks you have gone too far to be able to back out, suddenly changes the terms - in his favour, naturally.
In this case, the agreed deal was that, for £200,000, he would receive a 40% shareholding in Marcos. A £30,000 deposit was paid; Jem used this to build a much more upmarket stand for the Birmingham Motor Show than the company could have afforded otherwise, and this proved very successful for Marcos. Mr 'B' then came down to the works a couple of times and helped with the reorganisation of the stores and the shop floors. This was followed by a final meeting at an hotel at Heathrow airport, during which it was agreed by all parties to proceed. Two weeks later, Jem got a phone call from Mr 'B' asking for another meeting at Heathrow. Here, Mr 'B' told Jem that, unless he could have 51% of the company, thereby effectively taking control from Jem, he was not going to invest the balance of the money due. Jem said that if this was to be the deal, he would need a service contract. The reply was that there would be none; in fact, there would be no position for Jem at all. This was a remarkably stupid comment for anyone to make: Jem *is* Marcos; without him, it would be nothing. But he also reckoned without Jem; although the company was in urgent need of capital, Jem would rather have been bankrupted than give in to such obvious blackmail. The deposit had to be refunded but, in the end, an agreement was made to repay it free of interest on a monthly instalment basis. Again, Jem came out on top by getting an interest-free loan for his Motor Show stand, the extra sales from which allowed him to keep trading until the right investor was found.

Jem's son Chris, who also works in the company, has had his first experience of tricksters. Mr 'D' phoned him from Holyhead. He was, he said, in the fashion cutting business and, although he was at this stage primarily after a Mantara, he might want to place an order for a second car and, further, wanted to discuss the possibility of a dealership for Ireland.
Chris went to Holyhead to meet Mr 'D', who turned out to be of mixed race and well-dressed. Mr 'D' took him in his chauffeur-driven car to look at the premises which he had already earmarked for a showroom.

Here, he learnt the full story. Mr 'D' was dying of a mystery disease and warned Chris that this meant he would be difficult to contact for periods of time while he was undergoing treatment. He had no family and he relied heavily on his secretary and cutter to run his business while he was away; he could not afford to lose her which was why he was buying her a car.
Before Chris left, Mr 'D' signed orders for two cars. Payment was to be by a substantial VAT rebate imminently expected but, in the meantime, he showed Chris a copy of a large Swiss bank account.
It is company policy not to proceed past the body/chassis stage until the customer has paid his deposit. For a while, Mr 'D' kept giving promises but, as the money was never forthcoming, the company took the precaution of allocating the body/chassis units to the next customer in line while Chris, finding that he could no longer contact Mr 'D', took his enquiries to the Holyhead police, only to be met with the response: 'Not him again!' So far as their enquiries had led them, Mr 'D' had arrived in town on a pushbike. Despite this, he was plausible enough to convince local people that he was a high-flying businessman just waiting for his funds to come through. On the strength of this, he managed to borrow money from several people without giving any receipts. In order to gain access to premises, he borrowed keys from local estate agents to look round with a view to renting or buying, had copies cut, returned the originals to the estate agent then used his copies to gain access at will. He then engaged local builders and decorators (who, of course, were never paid) to start work on the premises so that he could impress visiting clients and potential investors.
It also turns out that Mr 'D' is wanted by police forces all over the UK for pulling a similar trick.
Once again, Marcos lost nothing. Even the brochures and a framed picture which Chris had sent him were recovered; the police found them in one of the premises Mr 'D' had used.

As for the chauffeur, he was using his own car and petrol. He also was never paid.

•~~~•~~~•

In 1990, Philip Hulme, a successful businessman, bought a Spyder, thereby achieving a lifelong ambition to own a Marcos. Realising Philip's enthusiasm for the marque, Jem approached him with an opportunity to invest in the company through the government Business Expansion Scheme and a deal was struck. With Philip's continued support, the company was then able to obtain the vital type approval and develop the production of the Mantara, as well as embarking on a professional racing programme for the LM 500 and 600.

●~~~●~~~●

***Barry Sewell competes in the Donnington round of the FIA Championship, in his Volvo 1800 Marcos*** (Courtesy John Gaisford)

To beat the recession, the company decided to diversify its product range into the cheaper end of the market. So, in 1991, it relaunched the Mini Marcos and followed this up with the Martina Coupé and Spyder. Like the word Mantula, Martina is a corruption of two words: Marcos and Cortina. As you might expect, it was designed to take parts from the Ford Cortina, in this case the Marks 4 and 5. Peculiarly in the business, Marcos now had models which appealed right across the economic spectrum. Although the Mini Marcos had been specifically produced as a budget car, the company had until now resisted designing the upmarket Marcos on the basis of cost rather than quality; indeed, its model at the time was as expensive as an 'E' Type. But the time had come to be realistic to market needs and the Martina was the first low-cost build classic Marcos.

The result of these moves was that, at the height of recession, sales doubled without any compromise on the quality of the Mantula being necessary. The company had fought its way upwards when most small series producers were having to retrench, by making sure that the range of cars it offered meant it could respond instantly to fluctuations in changing demands and economic conditions.

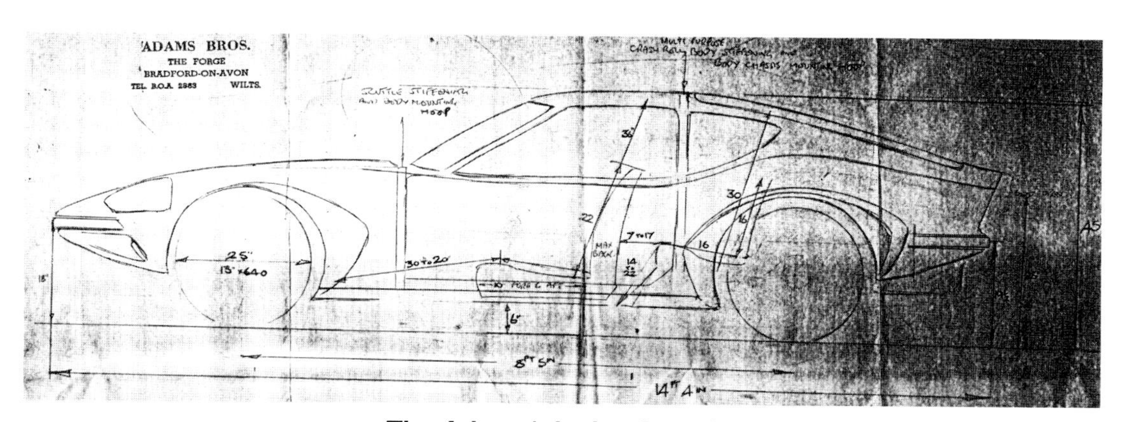


***The Adams' design for a 2+2***

Throughout this very difficult period, the Marcos racing successes continued. In fact, the Classic Sportscar Championship became something of a Marcos benefit: every year from 1986 to 1993 saw at least one class champion, with 1992 and 1993 seeing champions in two different classes: Roy Eaton and Jem himself. Together with Roger Ealand and Barry Sewell, they amassed between them 11 class championship wins, five seconds and three thirds. 1990 also saw Dave Bennett win his class in the Novices Championship.

In 1994, bringing us up to date, Dave Methley again put Marcos back on top by winning both the Classic Car Championship and the FIA GTS race outright, a very creditable performance considering the quality of the opposition. Dave has now become the acknowledged expert on early Marcos cars and looks after several of the Historic racing machines competing both in this country and overseas.

***Dave Methley, winner of the 1994 Historic Sportscar Championship, closely followed by Roy Eaton*** (Courtesy Fred Scatley)

# CHAPTER 12

# JEM MARSH, THE MAN

Small series car producers are men cast in the now unfashionable heroic mould of people who refuse to be beaten in the pursuit of their vision. This attribute can be seen in Jem's own life. Although the styling which is the Marcos hallmark can only have been the result of a vision created by Dennis Adams, it was given birth to by Jem and even Dennis agrees that it is Jem's pursuit of that dream which has kept the vision stronger than ever after 35 years, despite the company collapsing twice. Others may have thought Marcos was dead but they forgot to tell Jem. He knew it was still alive; it was just a question of how............So just what is Jem like and what is the character of the man who has been the catalyst, the motivating force, behind the survival and success of the company?

Now, in 1995, on the eve of his 65th birthday, he is undoubtedly one of the senior people in the industry and one of the best known figures on race circuits around Britain and Europe. He was chairman of the Historic Sports Car Club during a very successful three years for it, and is a leading light in the SMMT (Society of Motor Manufacturers and Traders) Specialist Car Group.

I first met Jem in 1991 when I was searching for a car more befitting the public image of my then expanding company than a much-loved but well-used Vauxhall Astra 1600. Although the Marcos had been a boyhood dream, it no longer figured in my reckoning because, like many people, I thought the company had gone into oblivion years before. But a chance visit to the Newark showground when the annual classic and sportscar show was on showed me how wrong I was There, to my surprise, was Marcos still very much mouth-wateringly alive.

That was me sold and it was not long before I went to the Marcos works at Westbury, Wiltshire to fulfil the dream of years before. Here I got my second surprise and the first clue to Jem's character. The image of the car makes it difficult to imagine that Marcos head office would be anything other than luxurious - perhaps a country house, even? - but that could scarcely be further from the truth: 'Head Office' and the works are in fact an extremely muddy yard surrounded by a series of apparently ill-equipped and dilapidated Romney huts with no apparent logic about them. To this day, after many visits, I still cannot work out how arguably one of the world's most beautiful cars can emerge from such surroundings. In fact, I wonder if the car is manufactured there at all. Jem has a legendary sense of humour and the sort of joke which would delight him would be to surreptitiously sneak in finished models at the back while customers aren't looking.

Jeremy Kearns, the sales manager, told me that the waiting list was six months but I wanted a car straightaway. The only answer was to choose a second-hand one and my shattered illusions about the works soon faded when he showed me a Mantula in concours condition. The company having been in existence for so long, it came as a surprise when he said that Jem Marsh was still very much at the reins.

'In fact,' said Jeremy, 'you are lucky he's not here now!'

'Oh? Why's that?' I asked.

'Because, if he was, *he* would have taken you on the test drive. The man's a hairily fast driver and all he does is terrify potential customers off.' He sounded rather morose about this.

I did meet Jem before I left, but only fleetingly. He obviously did not take *me* for a test drive because I placed an order for the car.

Although quietly spoken, Jem is a man of strong presence not entirely explained by his height. Although tall at 6'4", his frame is spare and he stoops in rather benign fashion due, no doubt, to spending too long in sports and competition cars. His presence, I found later, comes from the strength of a man who is his own master. On first acquaintance, one can be fooled by his outward diffidence but this hides an iron will, a focus and a determination to compete with the best without which Marcos would never have overcome the obstacles it has had to do to survive.

When he is on form, he is a man of great charm and almost old-world courtesy, characteristics which could be said to come out in his cars. However, preoccupation and a need to move quickly from one topic to the next, can make him abrupt. Like all people who pursue a dream, he is not a man who understands the word compromise. If he likes you, his warmth is immediate but he does not suffer fools gladly and, if he does not take to a person, his indifference is just as immediate.

If there is a single-minded business achiever who has not upset a lot of people along the way, I have yet to meet him; Jem is no different and it goes with the territory anyway. What is important is that, although he does have differences with people, bridges are always rebuilt with those who have made a positive contribution to the Marcos story, and this shows an underlying mutual regard.
He is a man of amazing energy which, again, is masked by his aloof, almost hesitant manner. As Lyn says: 'You can't miss him at home! He is always prowling around asking, "What are we doing next?" before we have even finished what we are doing now!' Quite apart from his motor racing accomplishments, he has in the past taken up stunt driving, ocean yacht racing, skiing, scuba diving and flying. He most recent interest has been golf. This may seem a mundane activity after the previous outlets for his energies but Jem does not play golf in the way others do. On one occasion, he chose the hottest day for many years to play 36 holes. But this was not enough, as Lyn relates: 'Jem did confess to feeling 'slightly' tired at the end of it, but he still had the energy to ask, "What shall we do next?" - while several others, including me, came down with heat stroke!'

His height, as reported in the press, has grown over the years in line with his stature in the industry. Starting as a mere 6'3", as consistently reported in all the early articles circa 1960s, he had grown to 6'4" (his actual height) by August 1984 (*Thoroughbred & Classic Cars*) but had shot up to 6'7" by November that year (*Fast Lane*), coincidentally the year in which the launch of the 3.5-litre Mantula suddenly forced the industry to take notice of Jem as a serious contender in the exotic car market! Thereafter, he seems to have settled down to 6'6" as variously reported in *Alternative Car* and *Red Line* (August 1987).

Jem comes from the same school as several other great British car designers and manufacturers - notably, in this connection, Colin Chapman of Lotus, but there were others such as Eric Broadley of Lola. These men were the result of two factors which in the 1950s conspired to encourage constructors: an onerous tax on new cars which led people to build their own from second hand parts, and 750 Formula racing which provided a cheap test-bed for these designs. Out of this hothouse of exciting ideas emerged several outstanding figures. Colin Chapman is perhaps the best known of these but even he has not stood the test of time in the remarkable way that Jem has. Sadly, Colin is no longer with us. However, Lotus is still a strong presence in the industry.

Although Colin and Jem shared the common ground of sportscars, from there Colin's interest took him towards single-seater and Grand Prix racing (in which he was, and Lotus have been, one of Britain's greatest standard bearers) whereas Jem leaned towards active sportscar competition. In that field, although Colin did race in his early years and actually drove in a Formula 1 Grand Prix, there is not another *patron* to touch the longevity of Jem's record, spanning as it does over 300 races in 40 years and, among many other achievements, winning three historic championships outright.

Jem is one of those characters beloved in our national consciousness: the gifted amateur succeeding in a world of professionals. He gets immense satisfaction from this. Many motoring writers over the years have 'discovered' Marcos as the most exciting car they have ever seen or driven. Yet neither the constructor nor the designer of this world-beater are qualified in anything. The chief executives of the major car manufacturers should be questioning why, with millions at their disposal, purpose built, comfortable premises to work in, the fanciest technology available and as many staff as they want, their design departments cannot even match, in comparative terms, a few guys with a few quid working in a shed.

As is apparent from the lack of pretension at Marcos 'Head Office', Jem does not play the part of the Managing Director at all. Most people become managing directors because that is what they want to be; Jem, I believe, is only so because that is the only way to achieve what he wants, not because he has any interest in the job itself. He therefore does not feel the need to surround himself with the trappings of position; indeed, he does not even have a secretary, never mind a PA. The offices of most managing directors are designed to portray how they wish themselves to be seen. A casual visitor would assume from the disused feel of Jem's office that this was a spare room used only when all the others are full, and is therefore a repository of accumulated unwanted junk (although it turned out in this case to be a treasure trove of historical magazines and photographs, some of which are used in this book). It is the office of someone who genuinely sees no need to have one and certainly feels no need to spend money on it. Jem does not work in an office, he works only from it. Nor does he feel the need to dress or act like a managing director. To him, all people are equal. Whether managing director or shop floor worker, people earn his respect not by their position in life but by what they achieve in what they do and therefore being a managing director is of itself meaningless.

It is no wonder, then, that he is no respecter of the Establishment or its figures: lawyers, bankers, politicians, government officials. In fact, he scarcely sees them even as a necessary evil. On one of my visits, he was about to suffer the, to him, tedious chore of conducting a female Euro MP round the works. He was actually more interested in her reaction to the single, barely tolerable, toilet on the premises than he was in any benefit which might accrue as a result of her visit.

The story goes that, if he did not think a person a suitable recipient for one of his cars, he would not sell them one. Jem hotly denies this but perhaps therein lies the real reason for him taking at least some potential buyers for a fast test drive - maybe these are people he does not want as customers in the first place?

An example of this is Jem's attitude to people smoking in one of his creations. Although the factory, like so many now, is non-smoking, he does not ban customers from smoking in cars; but he does class ashtrays as extras - and, on the principle of 'the polluter pays', which environmentalists have been urging on governments for years, charges the exorbitant price of £150 for them!

So what of the cars which have been his life? The Marcos has few equals as a road going car specifically designed for use on the track - or as a racing sportscar specifically designed for use on the road - take your pick. The main reason for this is not only that Jem has by far the longest and most successful competition record of any proprietor of a car production company, but that he also insists on using his own cars for daily transport.

Not only does this make the Marcos the only car to be personally used day-in-day-out on track and road by the company managing director, but it means that the company has not made the same mistake as so many others of compromising road performance for track use or vice versa. Of course, any road going car has to be adapted for the track nowadays but the Marcos needs far less preparation than any of its competitors with the possible exceptions of Porsche and Lotus.

There are three major British sportscars which might be seen as competitors of Marcos: TVR, Morgan and Lotus. TVR's ability to produce great performing road cars is as long as that of Marcos but where Marcos is unique is that the company still has the same hand at the helm whereas TVR has suffered from several changes of ownership and some unsympathetic handling. The founder, Trevor (hence TVR) Wilkinson sold out in 1963 to Burtons the Tailors, who set up a separate company under Arnold Burton, a keen competition driver and son of the famous Montague. But that has not been the last change of hands. As a result the design, while still beautiful, does suffer from some lack of personality. Peter Wheeler, its present guiding light, has done a remarkable job of rejuvenating the Blackpool marque on both track and road.
The Morgan, like the Marcos, has a shape today recognisable with its early models. In this case it was the Four Four which was launched in 1934 - well before Marcos - and making it the world's longest running production model. But no one could claim that the shape has the timelessly modern appeal of Marcos. When it comes to open competition, what successes Morgan have had in the last three decades have been in cars so modified from the original that they cannot claim to be the same car. Neither is it a good road car by modern standards; certainly not one in which you could drive for several hours in all weathers and arrive fresh for a business appointment at the other end, as I have frequently done in a Marcos. Having said that, the Morgan and the Marcos do appeal to people on the opposite sides of the same coin. Both appeal to individualists but the Morgan is more of a lifestyle statement than a car, the Afghan hound of the city dweller as opposed to the Marcos, the genuine working animal. Compared in this way with the Marcos, it sounds as if the Morgan is found wanting. It may be so for the true driver who seeks for the ultimate in driving

pleasure but then so is virtually every other car. But make no mistake, the Morgan is one of the great British cars. Founded in 1909, it has a unique place in history as the oldest car company in the world still in its original family's hands, Charles representing the third generation. Few of today's cars have real character. The Morgan has and that alone makes it special.
Lotuses are exciting but are not so successful as cars equally at home on road or track. While being excellent competition cars, this has been at the expense of their suitability on the road. There is a lack of luggage space and a more spartan approach to cockpit design - and not even the most ardent Lotus supporter could claim that reliability is excellent! Nevertheless, there is a magic about the marque which makes these problems unimportant to the marque's fans and to genuine car lovers.

***Mr. Wallace, who made the wooden steering wheels for Marcos cars in the 1960s, turned up at Silverstone in July 1994, complete with his two wooden bicycles!***

# *CHAPTER 13*

# *THE FUTURE*

The family connection is important to the future of small series car manufacturers and this book would not be complete without a mention of Jem's son, Chris. The decision for Chris to head up the sales side of Marcos is an important element in the future, and not simply for the reason of family continuity, although Morgan has proved how important this can be. Jem says of himself, 'With hindsight, the one thing I've lacked over the years is any real grounding in business skills.' I don't altogether go along with this as a valid criticism. Real leaders and entrepreneurs rarely have business skills which is why they are so successful; theoretical knowledge often limits vision and kills enthusiasm and initiative because it makes people act according to a set of rules instead of just going out and doing it. Marcos needed Jem's cavalier approach to get this far; what is needed for the future is Chris's formal technical knowledge and undoubted sales skills to back-up someone of Jem's spirit and independence of purpose.

Chris himself has already shown some of this spirit. He did work for Jem some while ago but, as Jem says, 'He was too wild and had to leave both the company and the country!' Is this not the pot calling the kettle black? Maybe, but that is good news for the future of Marcos. Too often, the results of strong entrepreneurial leadership by the father are ruined by lack of fire in the son.

Chris records that first effort of father and son working together rather more prosaically: 'I wouldn't say we fell out, but it was always a bit difficult working for him. Looking back, I can see I was a bit out of control.'

***1976, Father and son after a successful day in a Fastback and Gullwing..............***

***...............17 years on, Jem and Chris sharing the car at Coy's International GT Race, Silverstone July 1993***

This break, perhaps unintentionally, gave Chris valuable outside experience. The result was that, when he returned, he was able to make a positive contribution to the company in his own right. Prior to joining his father and straight from school, Chris served an apprenticeship with TT Workshops in Westbury, rebuilding old cars like chain-gang Frazer-Nashes, fondness because they both had chain-gangs. He then passed his City and Guilds. Subsequently, he built the first Group C sportscar for Tiga Race cars; he then went to the USA, where he ran IMSA and Indy Light Cars for three years. His cars had many racing successes including a class win in the Daytona 24 Hour race, a win in the Sebring 12 Hours and second place in the championship. On his return to the UK, Chris ran F3 and Vauxhall-Lotus cars for Christal Racing, before rejoining Marcos fittingly and, as he says, 'encouragingly', at Jem's request. He is now an acknowledged expert in suspension set-up, as any Marcos driver will testify.
Apart from this, Chris has already carved a long list of outright and class wins in racing, in some instances beating Jem's own best lap times, which must please Jem enormously. Among other achievements, he was elected one of the top six Formula Ford drivers in the world, coming 5th in the 1981 championship behind Ayrton Senna. Father and son now work well together, probably partly because Chris has reached a level of experience which Jem cannot brush aside, partly because they have overcome the father and son antithesis which can ruin so many filial relationships - especially with two such strong-willed characters - and partly because they complement each other. Jem commands loyalty through respect but this, by its very nature, prevents closeness between leader and led; Chris can talk to anyone and is instantly likeable. Jem, like all achievers, is impatient to get on and, therefore, inclined to intolerance; Chris works through diplomacy.
Given Chris's early exposure to motor sport, he would have either turned out as enthusiastic as his father, or he would have rebelled totally, as did his brother Nick, who became an artist. Fortunately, for Marcos, the former happened. As he recalls: 'A really special childhood moment for me came when Dad brought home an early Ford GT40. I was nine years old and just bowled over by this incredible thing sitting in our garage. But motor racing has lots of memories for me. I was carted around with Dad from being a baby. Once, he got so wrapped up in the racing that he drove off home

without us..........I remember we had a really great time once doing a long distance race in Sicily. That was in 1967. The Italians couldn't believe this English family turning up for a major international race with a Mini Marcos towed by a clapped out old VW. My mother did the timing. My job was to run to and fro across the pit lane hanging out the lap board and the Italians were yelling like crazy and cheering us on. Dad finished and won enough prize money to pay for the trip.'

●~~~●~~~●

So successful has Jem been in building the company up in the most adverse of conditions that it comes out of recession not only with type approval (and its German equivalent, TÜV approval), but two new major models as well: the Mantara and the LM500. The Mantara accelerates from 0 to 60mph in 4.65 seconds and covers the quarter mile in only 12.5 seconds. The LM is unbelievable in its performance for a road-going car, howling from rest to 60 in 4.2 seconds and with a top speed in excess of 160mph. Both can only be matched on cornering ability by properly race prepared cars. Stewart Smith may have been going over the top when he wrote in the *Coventry Evening Telegraph*: 'If you've ever wondered what it was like to drive a Formula 1 car, the Marcos can supply some of the answers,' but he does echo the layperson's idea of what a Grand Prix car would feel like. Leaving aside the heavily reclined driving position, taut controls, shattering acceleration and the roar of a V8 engine under stress, it is possible to generate high 'g' forces in safety even on the road - provided, of course that there is clear visibility round the next corner.
It is not performance alone which sets these cars apart - the quality of luxury finish both inside and out matches the best of the exotic cars and Marcos does all this for one-third of the price of some of them........These cars truly take Marcos into a part of the luxury and performance GT market covered by no other UK company, and few foreign ones. They are easy to drive, too. Viv Hart, writing in the *Weekend Telegraph*, said: 'I feel safer in the Marcos than in any car I've driven before.' She should know - she uses hers as daily transport to work. As Ian Hyne, the journalist, put it, it is 'docile to the point where your granny could drive it.' But this pussy cat is like a tiger; let it rip and it will roar into a driver's car *par excellence*. Its uncharacteristically long clutch travel helps together with the absence of a

turbocharger or 'cammy' engine, de rigueur among its competitors. A large, unstressed engine produces an attractive, relaxing engine note - the slow melodic beat of the V8. Turbos or high lift cams cause a delay in pick up; because the Marcos dispenses with these and relies instead on the old maxim, 'There is no substitute for horses', it has the best performance of almost any road car in third gear; this is, of course, the gear one needs most for overtaking.

But the real key to the future of Marcos is that the cars undoubtedly have that elusive 'X' factor. They have a curious, perhaps unique, appeal to the motoring public. I have several times been asked to join local classic car clubs with the comment, 'I know that your Marcos would not qualify you for membership but we would like to have one in the club.' In fact, I can think of no other car which, while thoroughly modern in style, is also seen as having a classic shape. The reason for this apparent contradiction is that the design of the first road-going model (the Volvo engined 1800) was years ahead of its time - but is now seen as a classic shape. There is perhaps no other car which fits in as well now as it did in its year of birth and which therefore has such universal appeal.

This appeal makes the Marcos a very effective promotional car. Traditionally, companies use Porsches, Ferraris, Rolls-Royces, Bentleys or, less opulently, Jaguars, BMWs or Mercedes if they want to create an image. Such cars can have a double-edged appeal: for all those people who are impressed by such exotica, just as many are put off by their display of ostentatiousness. I know from personal experience that my Marcos has never attracted anything other than admiration. Its appeal is on many levels; one is that it is seen as a visually beautiful object and not just as a car and, for this reason, I find it is admired by people not normally impressed by cars with, shall we say, exotic appeal. Writing in *Motor*, one well known test driver recorded that '.......it attracts attention like nothing else I have ever driven.' I cannot claim to have driven anything like as many exotic cars as he, but I can confirm, the car frequently having been cheek by jowl with most of the recognised exotic marques around, that mine is the car which gets the looks, and at perhaps a third of the price. The value for quality which the Marcos represents can sometimes count against it; although some potential buyers may find that it gives them everything they

want at half the price of its competitors, they may decide they want to be seen in something known to cost more!
The Marcos has tremendous appeal for people with an eye to beauty. But it is also for individualists who appreciate a car with character, eye-catching looks and stunning performance. Ever since the creation of the company, successive Marcos models have inspired what can only be described as euphoric, if not poetic, pieces from motoring journalists. Indeed, it is clear from reading many write-ups that they often cannot find the words to describe the experience of driving a Marcos. Yet, despite the unstinting and normally influential praise of the critics, and despite the obvious adoration of the public who will apparently spend all day admiring the car if you let them, this has not been converted into money changing hands. The only analogy I can think of is one of every film critic and the general public raving about Elizabeth Taylor and yet no-one paying to see her films.
But 1994 saw a change in those fortunes. The order books are healthier now than at any time in the company's history. Both the new Mantara and the LM500, the first truly exotic British car for many years, are catching the public imagination. The press is now even more in the Marcos corner and almost every magazine carried laudatory articles during last year. It seems fitting to let those journalists have the last say: 'The bottom line is, I fancy one.' (Steve Cropley, *Autocar* & *Motor*)-- 'Shattering Performance.....' (*The Daily Mail*)-- 'Hell fire........one of the quickest cars we've ever tested.' (Tony Middlehurst, *Top Car*)-- 'I didn't want to give it back.' 'As long as there are cars like the Marcos Mantara around, the rest of the industry can go techno crazy for all I care.' (Peter Tomalin, *Performance Car*)-- 'One of the most comfortable and ergonomically correct cars in the world.' 'The exhilaration of driving the Mantula will never be forgotten and must be experienced.' (Ian Ward, *Sports Car Monthly*)-- 'People will be forgiven for thinking that it is the latest offering from Ferrari, Lotus or Maserati.' (Steve Humphrey, *Bath & West Evening Chronicle*)-- 'Matches the best in world class performance standards' and 'It is a *British* supercar of which the world should be aware.' (Peter Filby, *Filby Group Publications*)-- 'Most cars reveal themselves in under an hour of driving, some within a few minutes. The Mantula will surprise and delight you for a long time.' (*Motor Sport*)-- 'It feels like a thoroughbred.' (Kevin Blick, *Fast Lane*)-- 'Fit to join the league of supercars.' (*Sporting Cars*)-- 'The interior has the high standards of finish

rivalled only by the most exclusive of cars.' (*Autocar*)-- 'Its ultimate tenacity is well up among the best of the supercars.' and 'There has never been a car like the Marcos, nor is there one now.' (Chris Rees, *Red Line*)-- 'I don't see a production manufacturer coming up with anything to rival a Marcos.' (Ian Hyne)-- 'One of the most exciting car shapes of all time.' (*Evening Mail*).

Philip Hulme's involvement has also allowed the company to consolidate its base abroad. This change in profile has been so successful that now 80% of production is exported - to date, to 14 different countries.

However, the main cause of optimism for the future may well lie in a change in public attitude. Government, corporations and bureaucracies have increasingly been forcing our whole way of life into conformity. Even supermarkets have educated our tastes into well-packaged, attractive looking foods which are a miracle of the art of tastelessness. Japanese car manufacturers have understood this very well and have been incredibly successful in selling us cars which, although undeniably well-built and high performers, are nevertheless the car equivalent of sanitised supermarket sausages. But there are signs of a public rebellion to conformity and a wish to return to individuality. If this mood continues, Marcos and other type approved small series producers will benefit.

If I was asked to sum up Jem Marsh in three words, I think I would choose humour, longevity and indomitability - the last two confirmed by the fact that, on the eve of the legal retiring age, Jem is still racing and both he and his company are poised to reach even greater heights. This is why it has been a pleasure to record the doings of both himself and his truly great British sportscar.

●~~~●~~~●

## *APPENDIX - MARCOS ABROAD*

Marcos has been a popular marque abroad, with over half the cars produced being exported. There are many enthusiastic overseas owners so this book would only be telling half the story without their say.

**Sweden** (contributed by Per Haegermark, who is also the motivating force behind the international Historic Marcos Register). About 120 Marcos cars have come to Sweden throughout the years, many of them being used for racing. The first car to arrive in Sweden was Anders Josephson's 1964 Fastback. Anders was a well known racing driver at the time, running a team sponsored by Caltex and consisting of his Fastback, a Ford Lotus 23B and a Lotus Cortina. The Marcos followed British tradition by winning first time out, at Ring Knutstorp.

Anders has another claim to fame: he must be the only person to have raced a Marcos on ice. The cars use special ice tyres fitted with long spikes which generate enormous grip. In the 1965 season, Anders came third overall in the Swedish Ice Racing Championship for Group 4 cars. This car had an 1140cc Ford 105E engine with a rare 5-speed Hewland gearbox - only five were built by Hewland and quite a few of them finished up in Fastbacks.

The Swedish Marcos Owners Club Racing Team (SMOCRT) regularly enters as many as 10 cars in various classes from Roadsports to Modsports in the Swedish Sportscar Championship and in the Historic GTS and GTP classes.

Two Swedes, Jan-Erik Andreasson and Johnny Lundberger, took their 1293cc Mini Marcos Group 6 car to Italy to compete in the Targa Florio. In fact, quite a few Mini Marcos have competed at Targa Florio, Enna and Mugello, mostly raced by British drivers.

Per himself has competed in more than 100 races over the last 20 years in his 1966 1800 GT, in the Roadsports class of the Swedish Sportscar Championship, in which he came second overall in 1989, and the Historic GTP class, which he won in 1993. Per's 1800 was also responsible for an award *not* won by him. In one race, the complete nearside drive shaft and wheel came off, caught at its moment of separation by an opportune photographer. The resulting photograph was adjudged the top sports picture of the year by a Swedish magazine. A somewhat aggrieved Per remarks: 'The photographer won a trip to the Portuguese Formula 1 Grand Prix. *I* won nothing - not even the race!'

***Per losing a wheel***
(Courtesy Gunner Johannson)

**Switzerland.** (Contributed by Bruno Meier of the Swiss Marcos Club). Because of the cost of obtaining type approval under the Swiss regulations, very few cars are now imported. Notable exceptions are the Mini Marcos of Paul Hofmann, who paid for his own expensive belt anchorage tests, and the Mantula Spyder of Tino Wüthrich, fitted with a John Eales-prepared Rover engine. Both owners are leading lights of the Swiss Club, together with Heiner Geering, the Club Secretary and Accountant - and, of course, Bruno Meier.

For a long time, owners tended to be posers who paid scant attention to maintenance, so many of the cars got into poor shape. Even with this rough handling, it is reckoned that only two have been scrapped, a tribute to the toughness of the marque. Modern owners are much more interested in getting the cars back to their original specification and the numbers of completely rebuilt cars are on the increase. Having said that, maintenance is a severe problem. The tradition of DIY

maintenance, so strong in the UK, is not the norm here and most garages will not touch specialist cars. Those that do, offer a bodged job at ridiculous prices; for instances, garages around the Zürich area charge about £54 an hour!
Given the problems of import and maintenance, it is remarkable that the Swiss club has over 40 members. Three early pioneers of the club are Bruno Müller (who used to import cars in the pre-type approval days and who founded the Swiss Marcos Team), Erich Jammerbund (a founder member of that team with his 1600 GT fitted with a Lotus Twin Cam engine and who is still a staunch supporter of the club), and Meinrad Schnyder with his 3-litre Volvo, who ran the club for several years and compiled the first Marcos register.
On the competition scene, the most famous event is the St. Ursanne-Les Rangiers Hill Climb, in which several Marcos drivers have competed, the best known being Michael Forsdyke.

**Belgium** (contributed by Jenny and Jos Vandervoort, and their son, Gunter. Belgium has an important place in Marcos history because it was the first country in which the cars were type approved, a tribute to the hard work of the Vandervoorts)..
Jos Vandervoort has a passion for cars. When he first came across the Marcos in motoring magazines, he decided that he must see what the chances were for getting the export rights to Belgium. Much against his wife Jenny's wishes, he came over to see Jem in November 1986. A deal was struck and two months later, in December, he brought Jenny over to collect their first car.
Jenny was soon won over by Jem, 'a nice man in joggers and trainers. He was living in an American motor home behind the Marcos works and it was there that we got a charming welcome, which even included a cup of coffee, when Jem managed to locate some clean cups.'
'Jenny,' Jos adds, 'realised that Jem was a bit of a lady-killer when he gave her a cup with a big, red inscription reading, "My Love!" But she wasn't yet convinced about the Belgium deal until Jem took her for a test drive in a Spyder - which turned out to be Jem's usual test-*race* as she described it - that her doubts turned to enthusiasm - which was just as well as it turned out. We weren't yet used to the UK and on our way home, complete with new Marcos, we got stuck in the middle of London on Christmas Eve!'
The Vandervoorts got to know Jem better when he went over the following August to compete in the Historic Grand Prix at Zolder. After the race, he entertained them in his motor home in somewhat abrupt fashion, by first of all congratulating them on

the preparation of their car and then falling asleep. 'Were the Belgian importers so boring,' asks Jos, 'or was Jem just tired after his race?' Probably neither: Jem has a habit of falling asleep anywhere.

In August 1989, Jos and Jenny held their first press show to coincide with a racing weekend at Zolder. Jem actually drove the ex-Jackie Stewart car to the event and then won his race. On that occasion, almost all the awards were won by British drivers. The prize-giving was held at the end of the weekend in the OTO Club in Zolder, where the combined weight of the drivers and their wives proved too much for the wooden stage and it collapsed. Willy Widar, the organiser, could not resist the opportunity of saying that Marcos drivers should be used to the effects of woodworm........

In 1991, Jos and Jenny started importing the Mini Marcos as well. To mark the occasion, that same year a Mini Marcos won the Historic Liège-Rome-Liège Rally.

It was in Belgium in August 1990 that Jem took his most famous 'scalp', that of Stirling Moss who was driving Willy Widar's 'Widi', a sort of Lotus 23B replica, in the Historic race at Zolder. To celebrate the occasion, the Vandervoorts managed to rustle up a band to play at the victory ceremony.